Thoughtfully Yours

This book is dedicated to my wonderful children and their children - Carolin

David, Sara

Michelle, Damien, ... ne.

You will notice throughout the ... ren have painted their piece and signed ...

To my other very special family in Stavanger, Norway - Einer and Mary Lynne Bergh, to whom I owe a huge debt of gratitude for allowing me the space and time over the last nine years, to do my work.

My team of helpers, for putting this together - Jacqui Mullholland (typing), Rita Anderson (Art), John Roche and Mary Hiney, C&R Print, Enniscorthy.

The cover of this book is an inspirational dream by Billy Woodbyrne, who has the gift of being able to clear Geopathic Stress from houses and spaces. When I thought I had my cover done I received a call from Billy to say he had an amazing dream and saw a vivid picture of the cover with a gold background, a rainbow and water - so I went with that and added the bridges of life.

A donation from every book purchased will be given to the "Share A Dream Foundation" who are not a charity but rely on public donations to help support their wonderful work with terminally ill children and their families.

> *This book is to be used only as advice, to keep you and your family well and healthy. Any unusual signs of temperature or serious problems should always be referred to your G.P., with whom you should have regular medical check-ups.*

ISBN 978-0-9560909-0-4

Published by Elizabeth A. Shaw. Printed by C&R Print crprint.ie 053 9235295

A Welcome from Elizabeth

The story of this book started way back when I was recovering from rheumatic fever — 1992.

I realised when working in the years before that people had no idea how their body worked inside. When we train in the medical area one takes for granted that people know and understand the mechanics and functions of the body - not so - I realised that medical books are so complicated and have so much detail, I started writing in simple form the Anatomy and Physiology etc.

The initial story is the struggle of the beautiful butterfly to release itself from the chrysalis and the beauty which unfolds, so there are butterflies flying through the book and the last page is a selection of butterflies (painted by me) flying into the distance — with the words ***"You too can be that butterfly".***

Then the story of the body unfolds — the structure and organs — where they are, what their function is, how life and emotional stress and toxic elements can make them sick, how to correct this with diet, herbs (all pages are coloured and all herbs & flowers are painted by the author). Lack of exercise, incorrect diet, processed food, sedentary lifestyle, emotional stress, sitting in the car and office all day, eating in the evenings and sitting in looking at TV is not a healthy lifestyle. Included are healthy diets for the heart, liver and intestine.

Taking time out too, is so important, away from the stresses of life, meditation and finding the inner self, how to find serenity, contentment and inner peace. Life now is so stressed, the simple life is gone, it's finding out how to bring the quality back resulting in peace of mind, contentment and serenity.

Mental stress, emotional stress, psychological stress all cause psychosomatic illness which manifests itself eventually as disharmony and disease, so Resistance — Repair-Recovery are the theme. This will be followed by another book of recipes for intestinal trauma. The Three Rs bring wellness, harmony, contentment and inner peace.

And so the story unfolds....

GO PLACIDLY AMID THE NOISE & HASTE, & REMEMBER WHAT PEACE THERE MAY BE IN SILENCE. AS FAR AS POSSIBLE WITHOUT surrender be on good terms with all persons. Speak your truth quietly & clearly; and listen to others, even the dull & ignorant; they too have their story. ❧ Avoid loud & aggressive persons, they are vexations to the spirit. If you compare yourself with others, you may become vain & bitter; for always there will be greater & lesser persons than yourself. Enjoy your achievements as well as your plans. ❧ Keep interested in your own career, however humble; it is a real possession in the changing fortunes of time. Exercise caution in your business affairs; for the world is full of trickery. But let this not blind you to what virtue there is; many persons strive for high ideals; and everywhere life is full of heroism. ❧ Be yourself. Especially, do not feign affection. Neither be cynical about love; for in the face of all aridity & disenchantment it is perennial as the grass. ❧ Take kindly the counsel of the years, gracefully surrendering the things of youth. Nurture strength of spirit to shield you in sudden misfortune. But do not distress yourself with imaginings. Many fears are born of fatigue & loneliness. Beyond a wholesome discipline, be gentle with yourself. ❧ You are a child of the universe, no less than the trees & the stars; you have a right to be here. And whether or not it is clear to you, no doubt the universe is unfolding as it should. ❧ Therefore be at peace with God, whatever you conceive Him to be, and whatever your labors & aspirations, in the noisy confusion of life keep peace with your soul. ❧ With all its sham, drudgery & broken dreams, it is still a beautiful world. Be careful. Strive to be happy. ❧ ❧

Max Ehrmann

The Structure

The Structure

The Anatomy of the Body

To keep it simple we will divide the body into eight parts :-

1. *The Skeletal System - holds you together – supports the body.*
2. *The Muscular System – weaves an amazing web around the skeleton and holds and supports.*
3. *The Heart and Circulatory Systems – consisting of blood and lymph.*
4. *The Brain – without which we just couldn't function at all.*
5. *The Respiratory System – cleans and oxygenates the blood.*
6. *The Digestive System – an amazing pathway through which all our food passes and which absorbs nutrients from the food.*
7. *The Genito Urinary System – filters and removes waste products via the urine.*
8. *The Endocrine System – consists of the complicated engineering of the glands.*

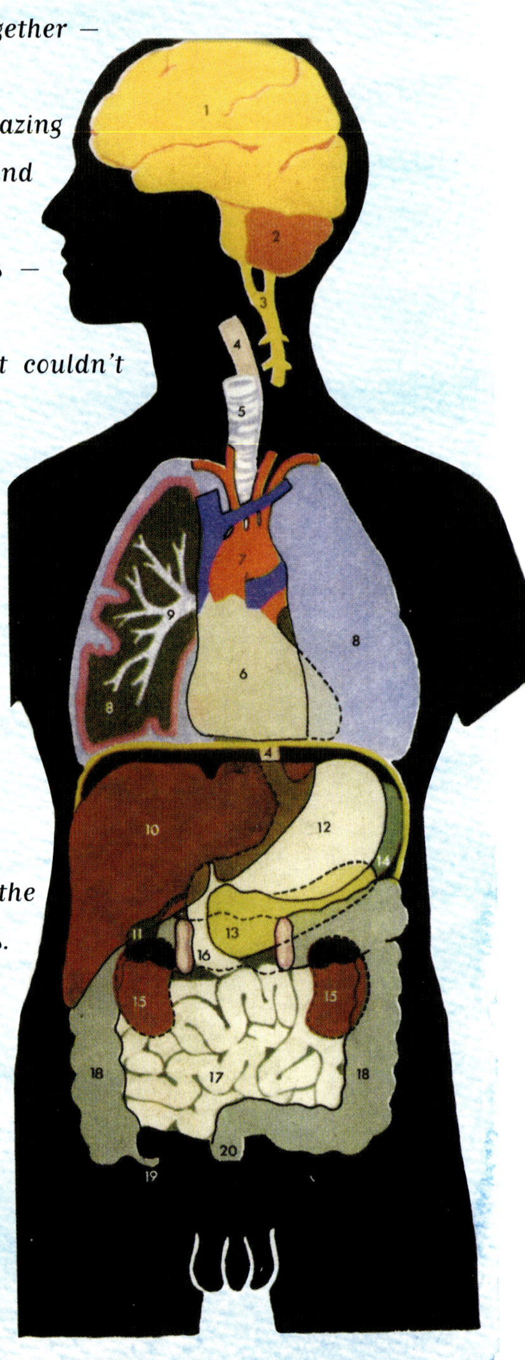

As well as these there is the Skin and other accessory organs.

Thought for the Day

'If we could bottle love, kindness and gentleness, and set it free all over the world'.

The Structure

A piece of divine engineering and a miracle of motion.

Thought for the Day

'If you carry your childhood with you, you never become old'.

Abraham Sutzkever

When you look at the skeleton of the human body it takes a long time to absorb the fact that it really does hold you together and protects the organs from injury – together with the muscle structure it can take a lot of punishment. However, on closer scrutiny all those bones contain their own supply of blood and marrow (in larger bones).

The skull, for instance, protects the brain, and from the various corridors of working area in the brain arrive the nerves, to every nook and cranny of the body. These nerves travel down the spinal cord, which is encased inside the bone of the vertebrae, which looking downwards from neck to lumbar – looks like a long tunnel. It is protected because of its sensitivity, and so every organ in your body is supplied by a nerve to the brain through a minute channel from the spinal cord to the tips of your fingers i.e. when you burn you finger, the message is gone to your brain (sensory part) quicker than you can get your burned finger into your mouth or under a tap.

This explains the fact that, where there is the slightest misalignment of the structure of the spine, the nerve endings are affected to the organs which the part supplies.

Even in a small baby reflux vomiting can be stopped by finger pressure on the vagus nerve (the nerve which supplies the stomach) by a qualified osteopath.

The Skeleton

The Skeleton acts as protection and support and facilitates our moving round by the action of the muscles and tendons, which are attached to the ends of the bones. The bones are made of calcium,

Painted by Alex Moran aged 17.

magnesium and a small amount of water. It is hard to believe that the skeleton is composed of 206 bones. Next time you are out walking or just going about your day, think about it! Inside the bones the red blood cells and some white blood cells are formed.

Thought for the Day

'Happiness does not come from what you have, or the more you want. Happiness comes from inside. It's up to you to go inside and find it.'

All bones can be broken or injured but the most severe is a broken back or neck, as it is these bones which protect the central nervous column. As life goes on, ageing begins and accidents happen, some pain and deformity set in, particularly in the joints, which are kept moving by ***synovial fluid****. This is a thick substance, which lubricates the joints. When accidents occur or a high level of acidity is present in the body, the synovial fluid is reduced or dispersed and you feel pain because the joints are not lubricated.*

"Fear, anziety and worry have a detrimental effect on the health. It is only logical to assume therefore that thoughts of happiness, faith and love will have a beneficial effect on the body".

Arthritis

Arthritis is the most common disease affecting the bones. 'Itis' means inflammation and in the case of arthritis the joints between bones become inflamed. This can be caused by wear and tear or too much acidity. If the cause is too much acid food taken into the body, then the arthritis can be stopped in its tracks before it does too much damage.

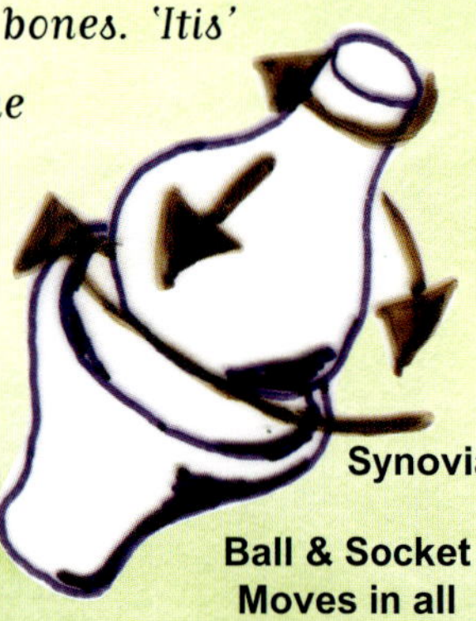

Synovial Fluid

Ball & Socket Moves in all directions e.g. shoulder & hip joint

Joint replacement has become very common and is very successful, but isn't it a pity that more people do not

Thought for the Day

Humility is a strange thing - when you think you have it, you haven't.

realise that the cure is in their own hands in the early stages. Yes, it can be corrected and quality of life can be restored.

It is very common to hear people approaching their 'golden years' complain of stiffness in joints, particularly in the mornings, and I get very disheartened when in clinic they say "It's my age. I have to live with it". Not so. That expression alone sets up a psychological negativity which is damaging in itself, and in turn affects the outlook and attitude of the person. Imagine getting up in the morning thinking "It's my age. I'm not going to get any better". What a load of old rubbish!! Do you see yourself in here? I'll bet you do. When I take histories from my patients, sometimes there are tears and dejection because their get up and go has long gone, and there is no quality to their life. What is there to look forward to but a downward spiral? Not so. I look at them and say "The good news is that you are going to get better". They look in amazement "I am, but how?" Mentally, the healing starts there. When I explain what is going on inside and the incredible power the body has to heal itself, a light switches back on in their eyes, their spine straightens up, hope steps in and a new chapter of learning begins.

The Ear

The ear controls both hearing and balance. It consists of three parts, outer, middle and inner. The outer ear is the visible flap which we call our ear. It is divided from the middle by a passage lined with stiff hairs at the outer edge to keep out foreign particles. It also contains glandular cells which produce wax to protect the ear from foreign bodies. This passage leads to the ear drum, which responds to high pitched sounds by vibrating faster and low pitched sounds by vibrating slower.

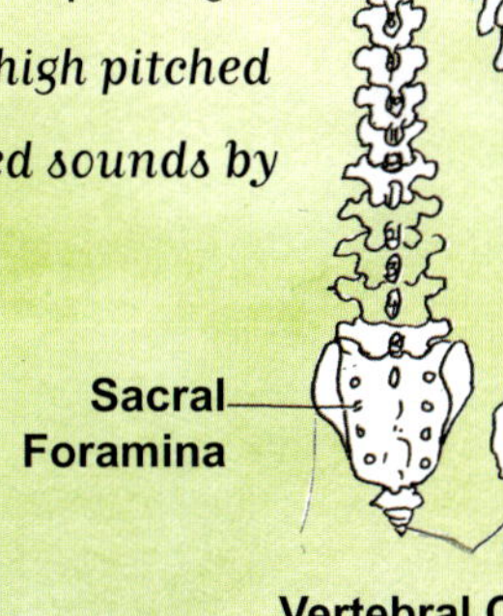

Vertebral Column

***The Spine** consists of 33 bones called the vertebrae, which* together form a hollow can containing the **spinal cord**. The spinal cord contains all the nerve connections to every part of the body. When the neck or back is broken, if the spinal cord is severed it will result in paralysis from the break area down. The brain sends impulses down the spinal cord to each part of the body to make it work, but if the cord is broken the message can't get through and the part can't function.

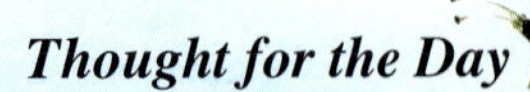

Thought for the Day

I grumbled because I had no shoes, until I met a man who had no feet.

The skeleton and indeed the whole body can take an enormous amount of abuse but a simple thing like misaligned vertebrae can cause agonising pain radiating to wherever the nerve ending is feeding. The **sciatic nerve** for instance travels from the lower back through the hip joint, down the thigh, through the calf muscle and into the foot. Pain along this track indicates that there is pressure on the nerve in the lumbar, i.e. lower back area. An x-ray is essential to determine that there is no trouble, and then gentle manipulation by a qualified osteopath will in almost all cases relieve the problem.

The back itself is an area where a lot of pain and discomfort is experienced. Injury or accident, bad posture, work related repetitive action or stress may bring this on. Unless an x-ray shows a structural problem massage, reflexology, acupuncture or osteopathy can correct everything else.

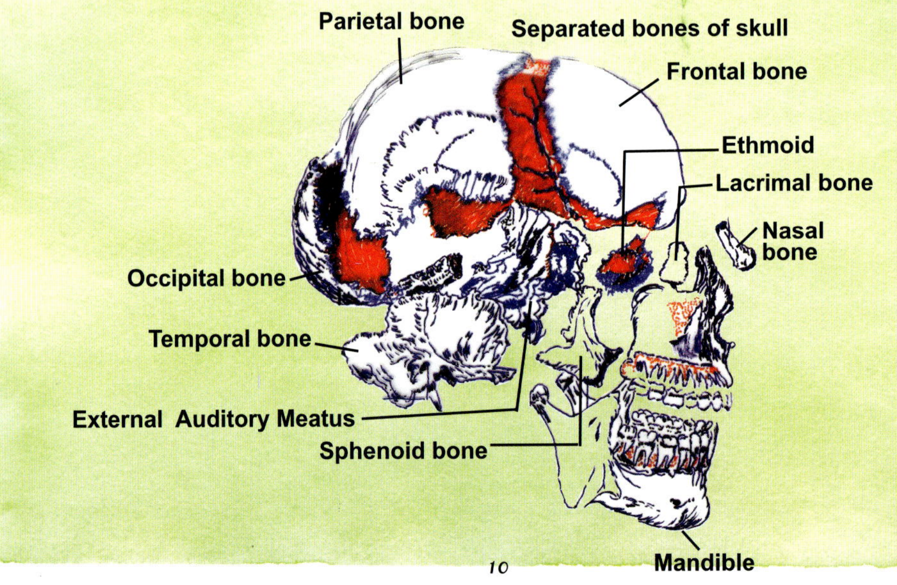

The Skull *consists of 22 bones, which protect the brain.*

It may be of interest to you to know that human and animal skulls are of a bone composition totally different from the rest of the body's bone structure.

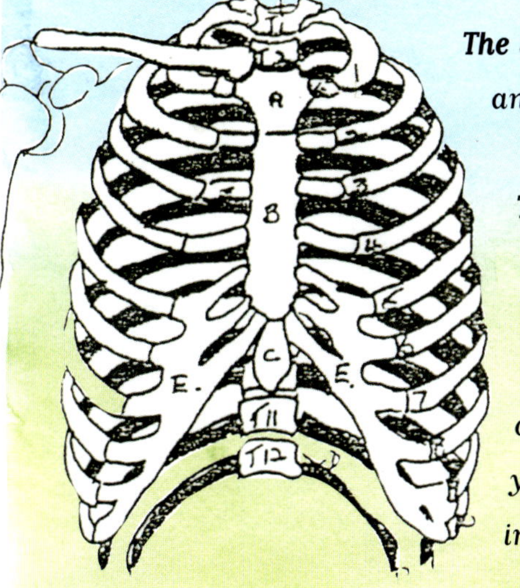

The Shoulder Girdle – *two clavicles or collar bones and shoulder blade.*

The Ribs *surround and protect the heart and lungs. They are connected to the spine at the back and to the sternum or breastbone at the front, except for the bottom two ribs which are called floating ribs. You can feel these if you put your fingers on your lower chest and side. An intricate web of muscles protects the ribs.*

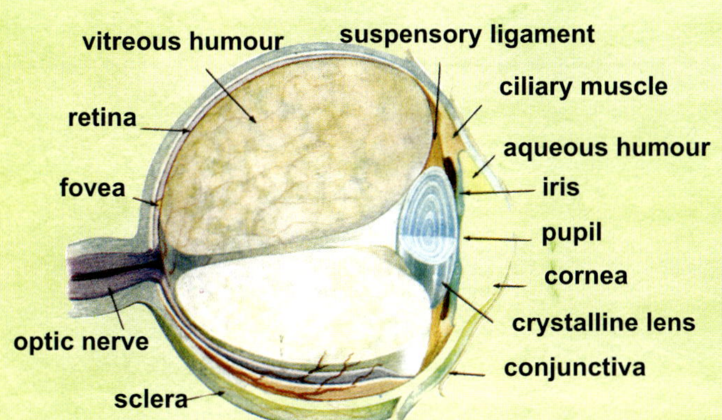

The Eye

The eyes are the mirror to the soul, study them and you can see the light, the dark, the sadness, the love, the trust and the hurt. Some eyes cannot see the beauty that surrounds them and some eyes have never seen because they are blind.

Thought for the Day

Do all the good you can,
for all the people you can,
in all the ways you can.

The eye is a miracle all of its own, you take it so much for granted, you wake up each morning and see a new day, the dawn awakening, the sun rising, raindrops on the window - rainbows in the sky, the beauty of our children growing from birth to adulthood, beauty as they say "is in the eye of the beholder".

Thought for the Day

We are all unique

When the rest of the body is well it can be seen in the eyes. A well balanced person who is content with life, without stress and a balanced digestive system, priorities in the right order, look in their eyes - "they glow". Sight may begin to deteriorate with age, cataracts, glaucoma, age related macalar degeneration which causes limited vision.

Treatments: Accupuncture, reflexology, eye exercise, eyebright herb - Lutein, Vitamin C.

Stavanger, Norway - True Story

Mary Lynne's Story: Over the last few years, Mary Lynne's eyesight began to deteriorate, quite badly, until she could no longer drive at night or see the text on television. On a visit to a specialist she was told she had cataracts and glaucoma but the cataracts must reach a certain stage of ripeness before they could be removed. Glaucoma is serious but can be treated to try and halt progression. When I was visiting I worked on the zones for the eyes and kidneys on both feet and after a few days work the haze began to lift from Mary Lynne's eyes - but then I left and came home.

In November 2007, I brought over an accupuncture kit, a beautiful piece of work, presented in an easy way to use at home. Mary Lynne continued to use this for a few days at a time and then a break - with continued improvement.

Charlotte Ross

Thought for the Day

Remember that great love and great achievements involve great risk

In March she attended her specialist in Stavanger to begin treatment for glaucoma - but her sight was almost perfect - he was speechless and couldn't believe what he found - "nothing" and of course he asked her what she had been doing - she told him.

This home kit and instructions are available from Aculife. This is living proof of taking your health in your hands.

Please look in the recommended reading at the back for an excellent reflexology treatment book and a colourful Anatomy & Physiology book plus the details of Aculife, +353 1 460 4962 or visit at www.aculife-ireland.com or www.aculife.co.uk.

Life lessons from a Snail

Steady as you go,
At your own pace.
No need to rush,
Life's not a race.
Easy does it,
Embrace the now,
Give yourself time,
You'll get there somehow.
Life is a map with different routes,
So enjoy today's
It's the one that counts.

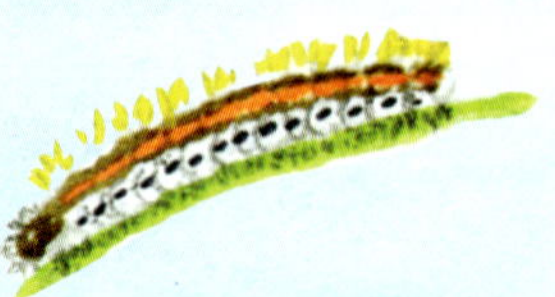

The Muscular System

The Muscular System

The body is covered, encased, protected and surrounded at every possible angle by a web of protective muscle tissue. It is elastic in that it stretches and contracts with your movements, allows you to run, walk, jump, dance and acts as a barrier to protect the bones of the skeleton from injury or damage.

Just stop and think, you take for granted every move you make, watch a small baby try to get the message from their brain to the muscles, to get up and move, another miracle of divine engineering.

There are only three types of muscle, the muscle covering the body, under voluntary control, the intestine is a smooth muscle and the heart has its own cardiac muscle. The muscle is composed of fibre and has a web of nerves running through, controlled by the brain, allowing you to do exactly as you want.

These muscular systems need to be stimulated constantly, particularly as we get older. The fitness of this system keeps us mobile and moving but allowed to weaken by lack of exercise causes aging and weakness to set in before its time.

The muscular system is also supplied by a constant supply of blood flowing through every fraction of tissue.

Muscular pain can be caused by a build up of lactic acid or injury. Treatment with massage and hot bath is very beneficial.

Fibro Myalgia - Fiber is muscle and Myalgia is pain, so pain in the muscles is very stressful and can become very debilitating if the cause is

Thought for the Day

The cure of the part should not be attempted without treatment of the whole.

From the Plato Chronicles.

I would wish to see massage available to all elderly people, there is nothing like it to ease pain and stress, along with exercises to keep the blood flowing.

Of course all continuous pain in joints and muscles which does not go away must be looked into by your GP.

Again I would refer you to a very easy book for your library which I hope you will start to put together, A Pictorial Handbook of Anatomy and Physiology by Dr. James Bevan. It gives you very colourful detail for those of you who would like to know more.

Exercise - Swimming uses all muscles and is one of the best to keep you fit and healthy, outdoor activity of whatever you care for, but remember to breath deeply when you are outdoors, to exchange oxygen and gases in your lungs.

Otherwise, dance, play golf, run gently, get a trampoline, do whatever keeps you happy, healthy and well, just keep your body moving.

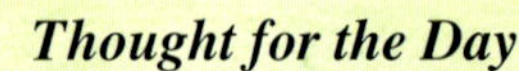

Thought for the Day

A true friend is someone who
reaches for your hand and
touches your heart

Chickweed - one of Culpeppers favourites

The Circulatory System

The Circulatory System

The Lungs

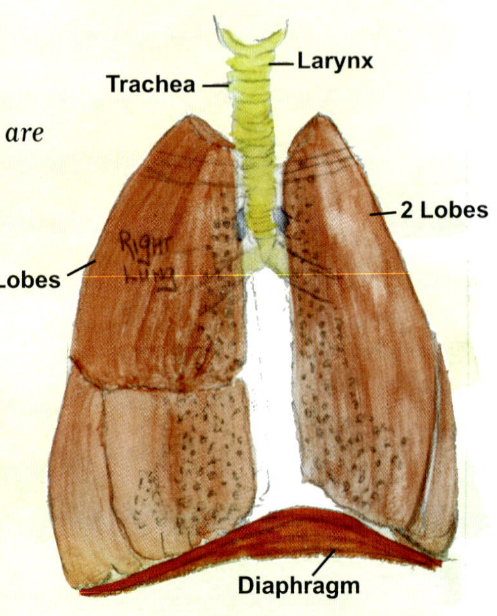

The lungs are situated in the chest cavity and are protected from damage by the ribcage. They are separated by the heart and various major blood vessels.

The left lung consists of two lobes and is slightly smaller than the right lung, which consists of three lobes. The whole object of the lungs is the exchange of gases. Through the lungs we breathe in fresh air, oxygen and exchange that in the lungs, and breathe out carbon dioxide.

One of the problems of life today is the amount of toxic elements in everyday life which we breathe into the lungs. The other problem is that we don't get enough exercise and inhale enough oxygen which is exchanged in the lungs and sent throughout our body, therefore breathing fresh air and oxygen to all the organs.

Coltsfoot

Lack of oxygen is one of the biggest problems of today. People are living in the fast lane and haven't the time or sometimes the inclination to exercise in the open air.

This causes stagnation and impurities to build up, not only in the lungs but throughout the body causing symptoms of tiredness, lack of energy, get up and go gone.

Thought for the Day

Hardening of the heart is more serious than hardening of the arteries.

The diseases of the lungs are Asthma, Emphysema, and Bronchitis.

Thought for the Day

'A positive mind means a positive attitude'.

Asthma and bronchitis can be treated but emphysema is a serious disease caused by inhaling i.e. asbestos, fungus from grains called 'farmers lung'. It is very treatable in the early stages but causes severe distress and can be very disabling in that the lungs ability to take in oxygen from the air is severely restricted by damage to the lung tissue.

***The heart** is the pump of the circulatory system. From the sketch you will see that it has four chambers inside with valves leading from one to the other. These valves allow blood to flow only in one direction from one chamber to another and prevent back flow. There is a wall of muscle down the middle to separate the two sides and to keep the venous blood in one side and the arterial in the other.*

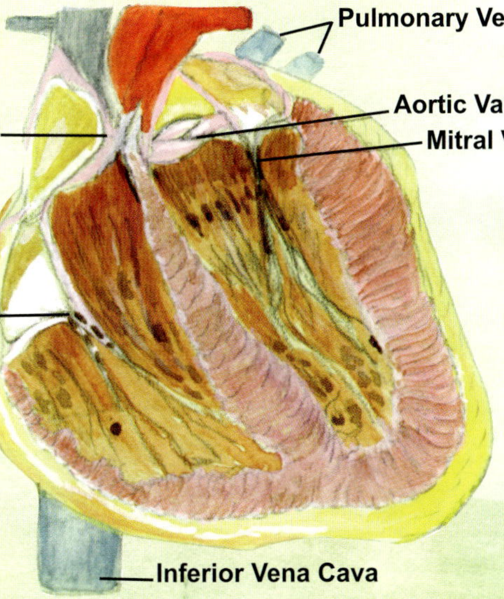

The heart is made of very strong muscle and lies mostly to the left of the chest cavity. In an adult it weighs about 255 grams and beats between 65 and 80 times a minute. The beats can vary widely; a healthy sportsperson can have a pulse as low as 55. Meditation can also control and lower the pulse rate. It's amazing to think the job of the heart is to pump 36,000 litres of blood per day around the body through a maze of about 20,000 kilometres of blood vessels. In other words - to every inch of your body and the surface of the skin. Take a look at the veins in your

arms and hands. There is a constant flow of blood going through those tiny veins non-stop.

Thought for the Day

'Don't look to the world for your peace of mind, it is inside yourself- only you can discover it'.

There are in fact two blood circulation systems. One takes the blood all over the body. It travels from the heart in vessels called **arteries** which get smaller and smaller as they travel until they reach the tips of your fingers and toes as **capillaries.** Blood flowing back to the heart is carried in vessels called **veins.** The second circulation system is the **pulmonary** circulation, which brings blood from the heart to the lungs to be cleaned and oxygenated. This is why breathing is so important. With the exception of people who take a lot of exercise or singers we don't use our lungs to full advantage. One seldom sees an athlete with toxic problems because they get rid of poisonous substances in the body by sweating a lot and by lung activity.

Foxglove

Back to the heart. One of the biggest problems with the circulation is the effect of cholesterol in the arteries causing restriction of blood flow to the heart itself. Bypass surgery is now a common treatment for this condition. Congenital abnormalities and damage caused by rheumatic fever and viruses are other common problems affecting the heart. If you are inquisitive and want to know in more detail about these topics, consult an easy

Painted by
Vincent Slevin
Age 13

anatomy and physiology book. As I said, I'm giving you just what I feel you need.

The Blood

The average adult carries approximately 6 litres of blood. It is composed of plasma, red corpuscles, white corpuscles and platelets.

Red blood corpuscles are made in the bone marrow and live for about 120 days in the blood after which they are replaced. Their job is to carry oxygen to all parts of the body and on the way back to the heart to collect carbon dioxide. This carbon dioxide is exchanged for oxygen in the lungs and the blood is circulated round the body again.

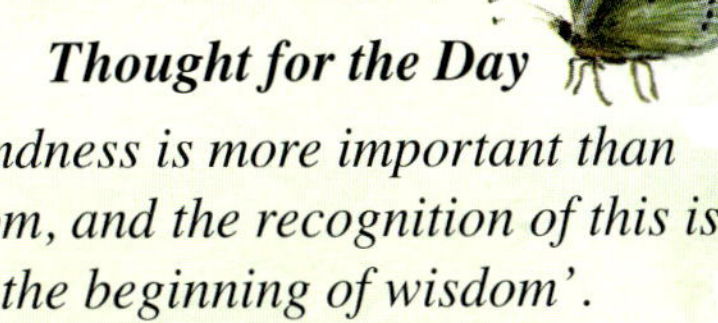

Thought for the Day

'Kindness is more important than wisdom, and the recognition of this is the beginning of wisdom'.

Theodore Isaac Ruvive

White blood corpuscles are the soldiers of the body and are also made in the bone marrow. If there is infection in the body the white blood corpuscles increase to fight it. When this happens the lymph glands swell indicating a problem, for example, the common sore throat and swollen glands.

Plasma is the liquid base of the blood. It is a straw coloured alkaline liquid containing many nutrients.

Platelets are the little cells which in their hundreds of thousands are responsible for the clotting of the blood.

Poppy

Cowslip

Did you know how blood typing came about? Karl Kandsteiner, while doing research on blood incompatibility in 1902 came up with the classification of A, B, AB and O types. Later on, A.S. Weiner, working on Rhesus monkeys found the RH substance in the red blood cells; hence we say blood is rhesus positive or negative.

The Lymphatic System

This is another circulatory system. Lymph travels round the body giving nourishment to the cells and in return taking waste products away. For example, if you burn a finger and a blister rises very quickly. This is caused by lymph coming to the area to protect it from infection. They are in clusters all over the body and swell up when fighting infection. In other words, the body is shouting for help. During a mastectomy or breast removal the lymph glands are removed from the armpit to locate and prevent further spread of cancer, because the infection could spread through the body by way of the lymph circulation. When the body is full of toxic waste the lymph system becomes overloaded and the result is a build up of cellulite on the hips and thighs. It takes a long time to get there, and quite a while to remove, so early prevention is the answer.

The whole circulation is in fact much more complicated but this is it in simple terms. I do hope it makes some sense. The next time you or yours have a cut or burn, if it is colourless it is lymph or red it is blood. You will know what it is. We take so much for granted.

Thought for the Day

'When making your wish list be careful what you wish for, you just might get it. If it's for you and it's meant for you, visualise it and you will get it'.

Take Time

Take time to think, it is the source of power,
Take time to read, it is the foundation of wisdom.

Take time to play, it is the secret of staying young.
Take time to be quiet, it is the opportunity to seek God.
Take time to be aware, it is the opportunity to help others.
Take time to love and be loved, it is God's greatest gift.

Crab Apple

Take time to laugh, it is the music of the soul.
Take time to be friendly, it is the road to happiness.

Take time to dream, it is what the future is made of.
Take time to pray it is the greatest power on earth.

There is time for everything.

Thought for the Day

Some people see more in a walk around the block than others see in a trip around the world.

The Holistic Approach

Nature is ever kind and for every ill of man she has a sure and certain remedy. She is a safe and strong re-builder of injured and failing constitutions and in such work, can accomplish miracles.

Basically there is no disease; only a sick person who displays some symptoms resembling more or less symptoms classified to our imperfect experience. The primary goal is to strengthen the patient's bodily functions so that they may follow their natural course and rid the body of whatever bacteria; virus etc. is present during the illness. When we use medicines which 'kill' germs, we can

Rosehip
Vit. C

never be too sure that they will not kill some useful and valuable little organisms in the body which are on our side.

When we cultivate the body's natural defences we cannot go wrong. Prof. Barry Commonor of St. Louis University, Missouri, said that man is more dependent on **NATURE** than ever before because technology cannot replace the full dietetic nutrients of natural food.

Hawthorn

HIPPOCRATES was the father of medicine, but his writings were codification of observations made from 500 to 900 years before his time. Hardly a decade goes by without some new discovery being revealed to prove Hippocrates correct; he too taught men to treat the whole personality, not just the man but the life and habits, above all to treat for the latent capacity of the human body to heal itself.

Thought for the Day
Loneliness is being unaware of the one who is with us everywhere

Illness is the faulty functionality of the body, indicated in the writings of Hippocrates and Galen.

Leonardo de Vinci (1452-1519) Artist, Anatomist, Biologist, and Aeronautical engineer. He made statements about nutrition that have a present day connotation 'if you do not supply nourishment equal to the nourishment departed, life will fail in vigour, and if you take away nourishment life is utterly destroyed'.

The Brain

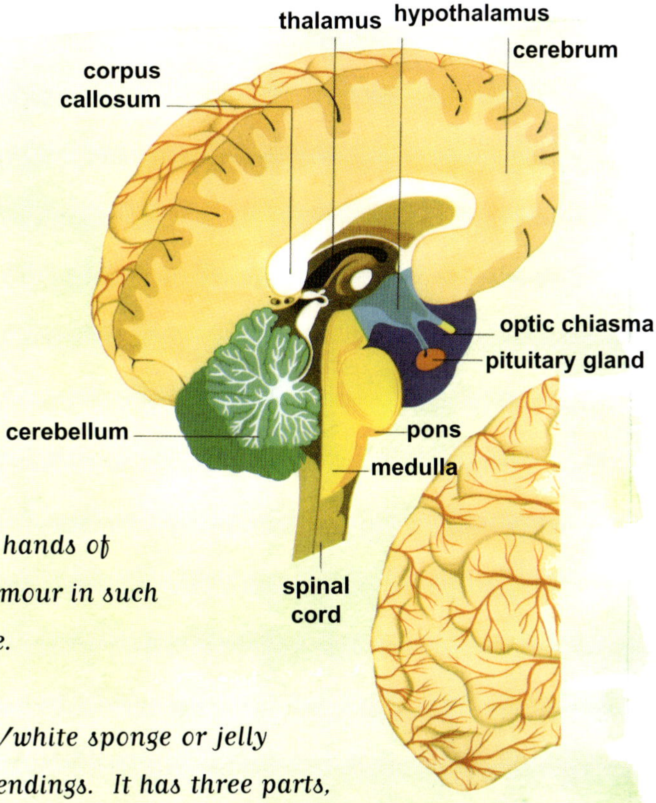

Now how does one explain in simple terms the working of the brain? I'm 'thinking' so my brain is trying to find a way to explain its make up. When I was a young nurse in training, working in the theatre, I just couldn't cope with brain surgery and yet it was incredible to watch the deft hands of the surgeon removing a clot or tumour in such a complicated web of nerve tissue.

*The brain itself is like a big grey/white sponge or jelly which contains billions of nerve endings. It has three parts, the **cerebrum, cerebellum** and **medulla** and is protected by three layers, the **dura mater, arachnoid** or middle layer and the **pia mater.** Outside that it is further protected by the 8 cranial bones of the **skull.***

My poor brain is still working its own computer to try to explain the how and why!

The Cerebrum is divided into two hemispheres, consisting of an outer layer, the cortex, also known as grey matter and underneath this the white matter. This houses the memory function, movement, senses and the higher intelligence.

Marigold

Thought for the Day

It's not the hours you put in,
but what you put into the hours.

Borage

The Cerebellum is much smaller than the cerebrum and located below at the back of the head. It contains both grey and white matter and controls co-ordination and balance.

The Medulla Oblongata is under the centre of the cerebrum and continues down through the central canal of the vertebral column as the spinal cord, which reaches down to the 2nd lumber vertebra. As I mentioned earlier, all the nerve endings are contained in the spinal cord and extend from there to each organ in the body. Again, if you wish for more information delve into an anatomy and physiology book.

To say that the brain is packed with billions and billions of nerve cells is an underestimate. They answer your every thought. You want to walk, talk, sing, cry, run, eat, do shopping, do laundry, your brain cells are way ahead of you, planning and activating. Every one of these messages is linked to both the sensory and the motor parts of the brain, and almost instantly the impulse is returned to the area to get its act together and get moving. All this happens in a split second.

Wood Anemone

When you burn your finger on the cooker, boy, do you get a shock? Your instant reaction is 'bleep'. That burn registers instantly in the sensory area of the brain which in turn activates the 'fight or flight' gland, the adrenal gland, which in its turn releases adrenalin and your heart starts thumping with fright. Remember, all this happens in a fraction of a second.

Thought for the Day

One can easily pick a wise man by the things he doesn't say.

One of the most common diseases of the brain today is Alzheimer's, a crippling form of early dementia often more devastating for the family than for the patient who is in his or her own world. A book well worth reading on this topic is 'Alzheimer's Challenged and Conquered' by Louis Blank. Another one is 'The Alzheimer's Prevention Plan' by Patrick Holford.

Wild Violet

Research has shown that metal poisoning and insufficient vitamin and mineral intake lead to this condition. More recent research has shown that lack of vitamin B12 and folic acid play a big part in brain health.

Think of the amount of pollution our bodies have to cope with. The huge increase in atmospheric pollution is a cause for great concern. This is due to fungicides, fuel exhaust, sprays used in the home, mobile phones and radioactivity and lack of minerals and vitamins.

Thought for the Day

'Aim for the best and you will find it – but promise to give something back'.

Yesterday, today and tomorrow

There are two days in every week about which we should not worry, days which should be kept free from fear and apprehension.

One of these days is Yesterday with its mistakes and cares, its faults and burdens, its aches and pains. Yesterday has gone beyond our control, it's passed forever.

All the money in the world cannot bring back yesterday. We cannot undo a single act we performed, we cannot erase a single word we said. Yesterday is gone. The other day we should not worry about is Tomorrow with its possible adversaries, its burdens, its large promise and poor performance. Tomorrow is also beyond our control.

Tomorrow's sun will rise, either in splendour or behind a mist of clouds – but it will rise. Until it does, we have no stake in tomorrow, it is yet unborn.

This leaves only one day – Today. Any man can fight the battles of just one day. It is only when you and I add the burdens of those two awful eternities - yesterday and tomorrow that we break down.

It is not the experience of Today that drives men mad – it is remorse or bitterness for something which happened yesterday and the dread of what tomorrow will bring.

Let us therefore live but one day at a time.

Thought for the Day
Don't let a little dispute, injure a great friendship

The Digestive System

Digestive System

The teeth

The Teeth, the Tongue, the Salivary Glands

On each side of the jaw the teeth are listed from the centre front as :

- 2 Incisors
- 1 Canine
- 2 Premolars
- 3 Molars

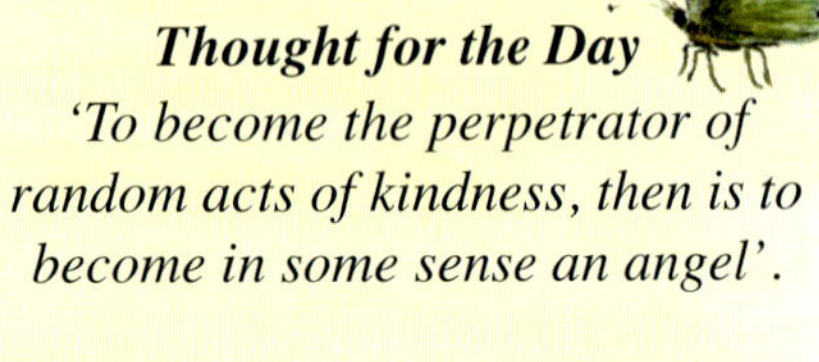

Thought for the Day

'To become the perpetrator of random acts of kindness, then is to become in some sense an angel'.

A bad tooth with an abscess leaks into the glandular system and eventually causes bad health.

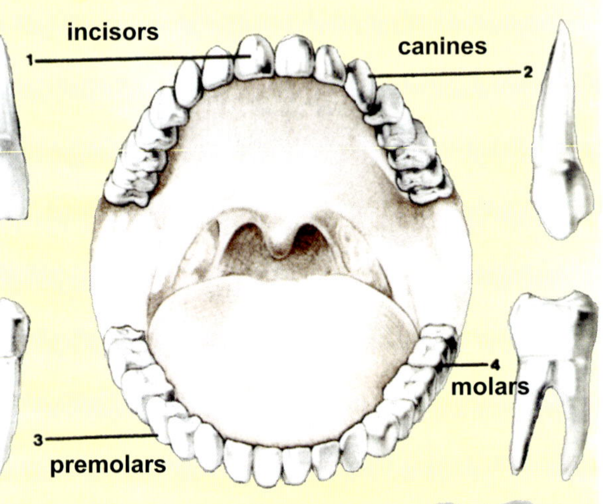

Did you know that every tooth in your mouth is connected to different organs and areas on each side of your body?

Chewing Your Food: This process is the activation of the glands called the **parotid mandibular** which lie below the mandible or jaw bone. These glands produce a substance called **ptyalin** which starts the digestive process in the mouth and breaks down starches before they are swallowed into the stomach, so would you and your family please make some new resolutions about your eating:-

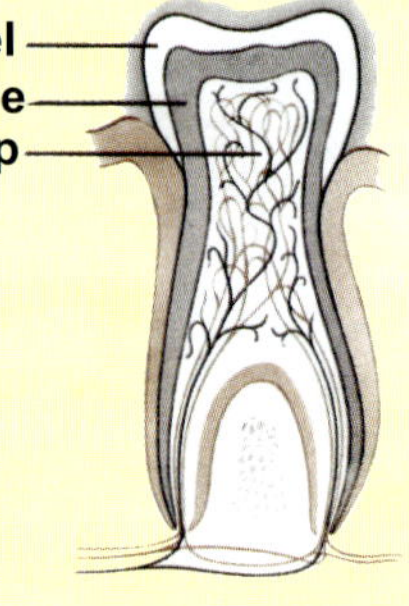

1. Eat sitting down
2. Eat food that pleases you
3. Take your time to chew
4. Don't drink until after your food

You will have a much happier tummy, believe me. All of us have got into the habit of eating on the run because life has become so stressful. But you can change all that!

<u>**RESISTANCE**</u>	<u>**REPAIR**</u>	<u>**RECOVERY**</u>
Detox, Diet, Organ rest, Water	*Diet, Vitamin & Min. Therapy, Tissue Salts*	*Exercise, Fresh air, Sleep, Healthy Diet*
↓	↓	↓
<u>**RESULT**</u>	<u>**RESULT**</u>	<u>**RESULT**</u>
Up days, down days, some headaches, weight loss	*Weight loss, energy up, mind and body recovery, bowel changes*	*Harmony*

The Digestive System

Sage

Before we even venture into the digestive system I want to tell you that your food digestion does not start in your stomach, no, it starts in your mouth! Your teeth are your inbuilt liquidiser. ***<u>Please</u>*** *chew your food until it is well broken up – why, because you have been provided with 32 permanent teeth for a reason. Their job is to break up your food as your tongue moves it around. Your* ***taste buds*** *are found in the papillae at the back of the tongue and also contained in the mouth are three pairs of* ***salivary glands.*** *When you see or anticipate a nice meal or even a bar of chocolate your brain stimulates your salivary gland and your 'mouth begins to water', as they say.*

All diseases start in an unclean environment in the digestive system. Unless food is well digested and daily evacuation takes place, unused food builds up along the digestive tract. This pathway is 26 feet long, and so it takes a long time to build up and boil over. This can be prevented, and I'm going to show you how.

Thought for the Day

'I don't know what your destiny will be but one thing I do know, the only ones among you who will be really happy are those who have sought and found how to serve'.

Albert Schweitza

But let's continue our adventure through from entrance to exit. The digestive system is not just your 'tummy'. It starts, as I said earlier, with

- *The teeth*
- *The tongue*
- *The salivary glands*
- *The pharynx*
- *The oesophagus*
- *The stomach*
- *The small intestine*
- *The liver*
- *The gall bladder*
- *The pancreas*
- *The large intestine*
- *The bowel*

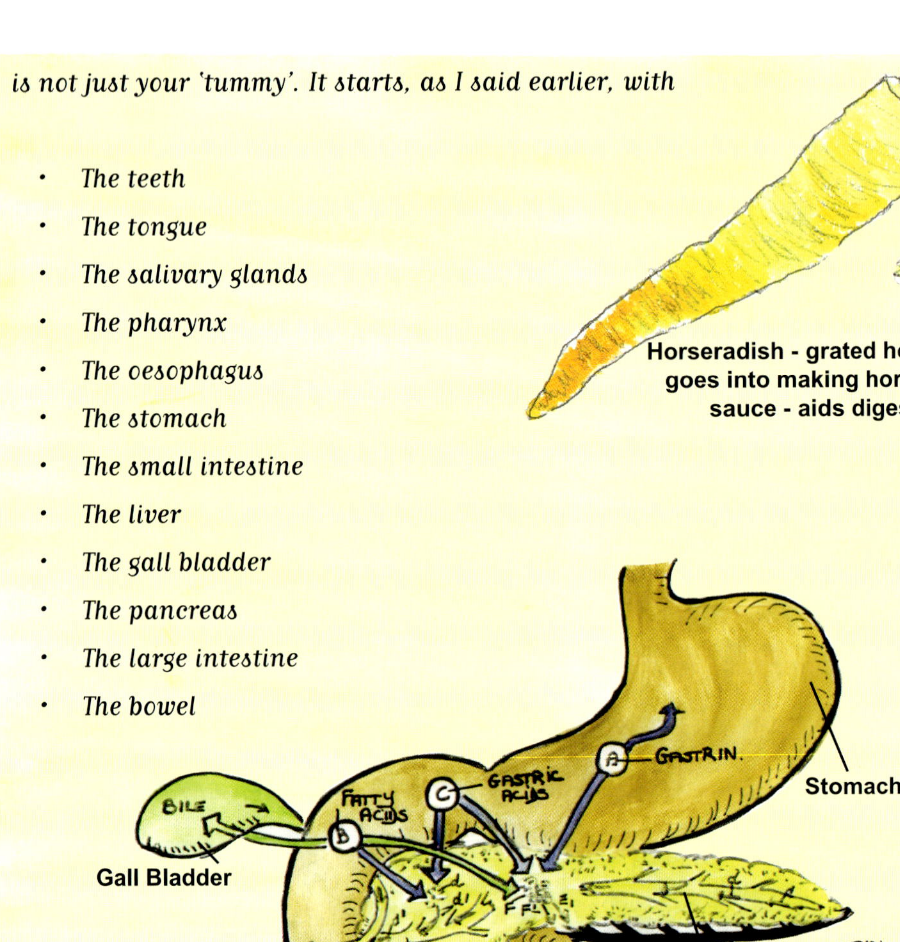

Looking at that list you will find your food travels a long way. The speed it travels at, **the metabolic rate,** *varies from person to person. Usually from entrance at the mouth to evacuation takes between 3 to 5 days (although there are people who only have a bowel motion once a week, which leaves a very toxic body).*

The food passes from the mouth down the pharynx, into the oesophagus and down into the stomach through a muscle called a ***sphincter.*** *This is a ring of muscle which opens to allow food through. It takes approximately four hours to digest food in the stomach. The lining of the stomach produces from its glands different*

Thought for the Day

'My religion is very simple,
& my religion is kindness'
The Dali Lama

kinds of gastric juices. **Pepsin** digests proteins, **renin** to digest milk and **hydrochloric acid.** If too much hydrochloric acid is produced it causes gastritis, a very painful stomach which can become ulcerated. The major cause of this happening is, of course, stress and eating on the run.

Thyme

The stomach is like a bag or sack made of three layers of muscle with two openings. The more you eat, the more it expands. The more it stretches, the more it needs filling. The more it needs filling, the hungrier you feel.

OK, so the food is churned up in the stomach, ground down by the digestive juices and after about four hours it passes into the small intestine through the **pyloric** sphincter muscle. The intestine is separated from the chest cavity by a strong sheet of muscle called the **diaphragm.** The **intestine** lies coiled up inside your abdomen in the cavity between your ribs and your **pelvis,** looking, if you will excuse the expression, like pounds of fresh sausages, quietly working and digesting your food.

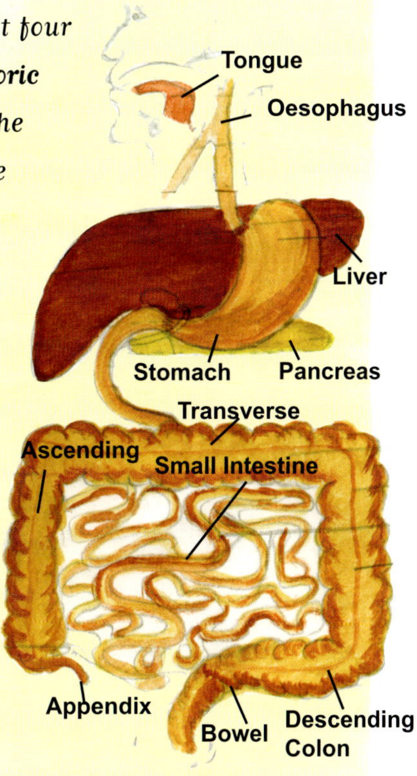

Tongue
Oesophagus
Liver
Stomach
Pancreas
Transverse
Ascending
Small Intestine
Appendix
Bowel
Descending Colon

The **duodenum** is the first part of the small intestine. It is here that ulcers are likely to occur, particularly in people of nervous disposition. The food passes by a very complicated process through the further parts of the small intestine, called the **jejunum** and the **ileum,** and then through to the **large intestine.** This is in three sections called the **ascending** colon which travels up the right

Thought for the Day

'Spread your love everywhere you go'

Mother Theresa

side of the abdominal cavity, the **transverse** colon which goes across the top, and the **descending** colon going down the left side. Food then passes into the **bowel** or **rectum,** the last stage before evacuation, which takes place at least once a day, we hope. In the colon the food is kept moving by **peristaltic** movement which is wavelike contractions of the muscles.

Parsley

In the intestine, apart from the enzymes for digestion we have approximately 3lbs of a natural bacteria. Its job is to help to digest the food even further before the residue is left for elimination. Today in many cases of digestive disturbance this bacteria is missing. The cause of this can be stress or over-use of antibiotics, which have a habit of killing off the good bacteria in the intestine. If there are no bacteria in the intestine to break down the food it just putrefies there, kicking up an awful racket inside and making quite a foul smelling bowel. Antibiotics can also cause Thrush as a side effect of their activity.

We all eat too much and drink too little – water, I mean. If you eat and swallow your food too quickly you are making your stomach work too hard. After your dinner you maybe go shopping, meet a pal on the street – let's go have a coffee. When you have a coffee you like something sweet with it, and are tempted by a cream bun. Delicious, yes, but your poor stomach is busy digesting your dinner and is halfway through and it gets a message from the brain to open up. "Oh, Bleep! We have only partly digested this lot and down comes more – OK, juices, we've got to work harder here, this human has no respect for a hard working organ". That is typical of what

Thought for the Day

'It is one of the most beautiful compensations of life that no man can sincerely try to help another without helping himself first'.

Ralph Waldo Emmerson

happens, and then you wonder why you have indigestion!!

Thought for the Day

'There is no university like the university of life '

Years ago I had very severe colitis (bleeding from the intestine). I was in bad trouble. I had dreadful pain and indigestion and had antacids everywhere, in my car, in my bag, the kitchen, the bedroom – you name it, I had it. On my road to recovery a very eminent physician/homeopath in Dublin sent a sample of my hair to London to be analysed. It showed that I had lead and aluminium toxicity in my body to the extent, as he said that I was spitting it out through my hair. I was intolerant to a lot of foods too, because my intestine was so badly damaged.

Cinnamon - eases digestion

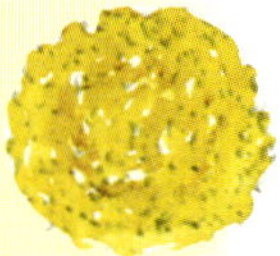

That was in 1981, and it has been a learning adventure ever since, and I'm still learning every day. All of you have played a part in putting this together to help other people keep themselves and their loved ones on the right road.

One discovery which amazed me was that the antacid tablets which I was chewing by the dozen to ease my discomfort not only altered the digestive juices but they also contained aluminium! So do the cooking utensils and tinfoil we use every day. I don't any more, its back to Pyrex and greaseproof paper. Finding the source of the lead was something else, unless it came from the water pipes, but we couldn't solve that one.

That was my introduction to complementary medicine. In 1984 I had the first vega scan, done by another practitioner who was way ahead of modern medicine at that stage, and was and still is brilliant in his work. During that

Mint

period I learned a lot of which I have been putting into practice since. It is all based on the power of the body to heal itself and knowing what makes it ill in the first place.

Nutmeg

If there is Dis-harmony in the mind
It creates dis-ease in the body.

Hence we speak of Mind, Body and Spirit medicine as they are all involved in illness.

Thought for the Day
'What goes around comes around'

During the entire journey though the digestive tract the goodness and nourishment is taken out of the food through the wall of the small intestine and into the blood. This is a very complicated process which we don't need to go into here. Just imagine all the waste which passes into the large intestine and passes through to the bowel to be excreted. So now you see why it is so important to keep your intestine clean and in good working order with good food, daily exercise, and plenty of water.

Another cause of digestive disturbance is eating too much yeast. Yeasts occur in bought white and brown bread, junk foods, freshly baked rolls, croissants, sugar, and of course alcohol which needs yeast for fermentation.

The good news is that the intense discomfort which accompanies this condition can be cleared up.
The diseases which afflict the intestine are:-

- **Cancer** – the biggest cause of death.
- **Ulcerative colitis** – severe bleeding and inflammation inhibiting proper absorption of nutrients and so sometimes causes malnutrition.
- **Diverticulitis** – painful little pockets of air develop in the wall of the colon.
- **Crohn's disease** – chronic inflammation of the walls of the intestine causing constant bowel flow.
- **Irritable bowel syndrome** – can be corrected very quickly with proper diet.

Thought for the Day

Never laugh at anyone's dream. People who don't have a dream don't have much.

Remember, what you put into your body is expected to provide heat, energy, repair, growth for the young and maintenance of cells. Proper diet keeps us young, good-looking, bright-eyed and full of energy. With the programme of detoxing and replenishing, one of the most rewarding parts of my work is watching the body come back to life. Remember the eyes are the mirror of the soul, and to watch the light switch back on is worth everything.

My father was eighty-six years old when he died. He was never ill, apart from having his appendix out. He hadn't a crooked bone in his body or a pain or ache, and here is why. When we were young I remember Dad with only a few teeth so he had to chew meticulously and mash up his food, with the result that when it went down to his stomach the saliva in his mouth had done its job well. When we were old enough to be allowed up to the dining table, Dad would still be half way through his dinner when we were finished, and this was his way until he was an old man. Supper was similar, and then a full tumbler of milk with buttered Marietta biscuits before retiring by the fire.

Somewhere along the way he did acquire a good set of dentures, but his habit never changed, not only that but he ate full cream, ice cream, eggs and sugar daily, but his digestion was perfect. A lesson to be learned. My mother was a superb cook and that played a part too, and the diet included a lot of game, rabbit, fish, pheasant, snipe etc. which were all healthy protein and all home grown veg and fruit (apples, peaches, strawberries, raspberries, gooseberries and rhubarb).

Milkthistle

Symptoms of digestive disorder:

- *Get up and go has gone.*
- *Loss of energy*
- *Bloating in abdominal area*
- *Wind*
- *Heartburn*
- *Burping*
- *Irregular bowel habits*
- *Fuzzy brain (lack of brain energy)*

Thought for the Day

'Remember when you come into this life you are not here to take, you are here for a reason- to create, to do a job, for a reason. But most of all, as you go through life you learn, as you work you achieve – give something back'.

If you have these symptoms, then they are easily corrected by diet. However, it is always a very good idea to have your G.P. check you out for other problems first. Symptoms like this take a long time to build up in the system before becoming a constant problem which if not checked and corrected will lead to loss of quality of life, grumpiness, irritability, exhaustion, unwellness and weight gain. But, a few weeks on a corrective diet and replacement of proper nutrients never fails to get results. It means taking away certain foods which cause accumulative problems, give the main organs a rest – God knows they need it!

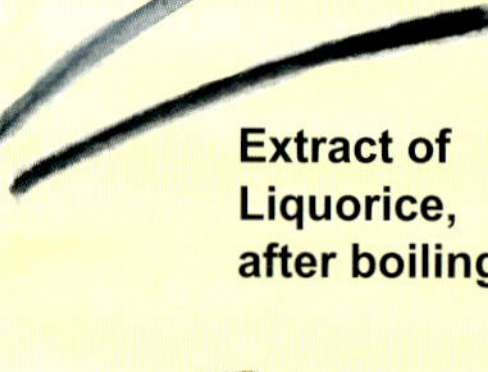

Extract of Liquorice, after boiling

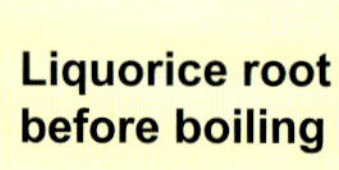

Liquorice root before boiling

Foods to avoid – anything that moulds in the fridge, all sugars and sweeteners, all tinned and packet food, all processed foods, soft drinks, all additives and preservatives, all flavourings, all yeast breads and yeast products, all alcohol, particularly beers and wine because they are fermented and they can be a big factor in digestive disturbance. This does not mean it is a permanent problem, but one which needs to be addressed and corrected.

Dandelion

Modern foods, all freshly baked bread, bagels, croissants and all rolls, breads with yeast, taken on a regular basis cause problems in the gut.

Normally when the stomach passes churned food called 'Chime' into the next part of the digestive process, the duodenum, the absorption of the nutrients starts.

The residue is passed on to the large intestine and bowel, where it is waste matter and should be passed daily to rid the body of what is residual waste.

It is when this process does not happen that the body becomes toxic and sick, and disease steps in and breaks down the system. Don't allow it to happen to you!

Herbs which aid digestion: Sage, parsley, thyme, fennel, rosemary, oregano, cayenne pepper.

Our stomach lining produces three different juices to aid in the digestion of foods. In times of stress or in the elderly these juices may be impaired or restricted. A good replacement is needed. Udo's digestive enzymes are available all over, plus

Mullein

Thought for the Day

'Work like you do not need the money,
love like you have never been hurt.
Dance like nobody is watching.
Sing like nobody is listening.
Live like it is Heaven on Earth'.

sauerkraut as a natural ferment for the bowel on the continent, but is available here in health food shops. Acidophilus, a natural product or probiotic – corrects the imbalance.

Organic apple cider vinegar, taken daily, keeps the acid and alkaline balance correct.

capsicum

Babies problems

Symptoms:

Cramping pain, diarrhoea, food passing through very quickly, strong odour from bowel motion, distended abdomen, wind, rash, sleepless nights.

- *rule out colic disease, lactose intolerance.*

Natural intestinal bacteria which is in the intestine and its job is to digest food which is passed from the stomach is destroyed by the use of antibiotics. This then causes discomfort and bloating when the food putrefies because there is no natural bacteria to digest it and pass it on to the next part of the bowels. It is very easily corrected by corrective therapy and diet and perhaps a change of formula.

Today, with modern diet problems and yeast infection the baby carries the yeast infection through from the womb so it is very easy to correct mother and baby at the same time.

Common Mallow

If you can think of nothing for which to give thanks you have a poor memory.

So now we have woven our way through the stomach and intestines, don't think for a minute that we are finished! The other organs which play an important part in assisting digestion are:-

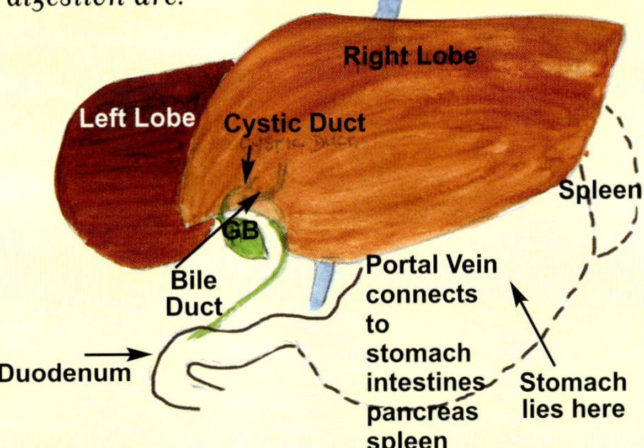

- *The Liver*
- *The Gall Bladder*
- *The Pancreas*

*The **liver** is the biggest organ in the body. It has some job to do to detox everything that is taken into the body. If you put your hand on your right side just at the waist line from side to middle, that is where your liver rests and works. It weighs approximately 1.5 kilos and is divided into four **lobes** of differing sizes. Without going into too much detail, it breaks everything down into harmless substances, digests carbohydrates and turns it into **glycogen** for energy. Often later in life, with prolonged use of drugs, inhalers, antibiotics, overuse of alcohol and toxic elements of life it becomes laden and sad, hence the term 'feeling liverish'. The liver also stores blood and vitamins and produces other substances, bile being the one you recognise from gall bladder problems.*

Blueberry - Vit. C

*The liver passes bile into the **gall bladder,** which in turn passes it through the **bile duct** into the digestive tract to break down fats. A troubled gall bladder can cause a lot of problems and make one very nauseated and sick. Chronic problems of this nature are resolved by diet first, then, if necessary, surgery.*

Thought for the Day

'The quality of mercy is not strained,
it dropeth as the gentle rain from
heaven upon the place beneath, it is
twice blessed; it blesseth him that
giveth and him that takes'.
William Shakespeare

The liver also needs to be kept free of toxins and over load. I'm going to tell you how. You will be amazed how you can take responsibility for how you feel and your family too, although I have found from experience that one must be at a very low ebb oneself to appreciate just how good it is to feel well again, and without drugs. There is no point in telling others who feel ok anyway because :

1. They don't understand what it is like, and
2. They have constitutions like oxen, and don't understand what it is like to feel so ill every day.

There are people like that, and they are to be envied.

Thought for the Day

'Few people give to their bodies as much time and care as they bestow upon mechanical appliances'.

Ancient Chinese Proverb

Each one of us is an individual, and must take responsibility for **wellness.**

There is no point in saying it works like ABC, it doesn't. We each have a unique metabolism (digestive process) and each works according to its own likes and dislikes. Every single person is a unique individual in his own right and has his own unique digestive system. For example, some people prefer warm food, some can thrive on cold food, some on vegetarian and others on a macrobiotic diet. Junk foods and processed foods eaten in moderation are ok, but on a continual basis cause major problems. Each and every one must experiment with food and see and know what suits his or her own system and leave out that which doesn't. The strongest reactions and causes of problems are:-

- Wheat
- Dairy produce
- Caffeine
- Potato
- Yeast Infection
- Parasitic infection
- Bacterial infection

- Viral infection
- Lack of exercise
- Stagnation

Wild Rose

These are the biggest causes of complaints such as tiredness, irritable bowel syndrome, get-up-and-go gone, inability to deal with work or chores, no quality of life. Each of these symptoms is caused initially by a breakdown in and lack of vitamins, minerals and essential fatty acids. God provided a cure in nature for everything, and it costs very little. It's just a matter of knowing what it is.

Liver – dandelion, beetroot. A daily fast on juices and salad once a week is a very good thing, especially in conjunction with bowel cleansing with a herbal product. This gives organs a rest, and a chance to regenerate.

We all go on holiday to rest and recuperate; give your inside a chance as well. It pays large dividends in extended youthfulness, no aches and pains, increase in energy and better quality of life.

Chrysanthemum

The highest goodness is like water
Water benefits all things and does not compete
It stays in the lowly places which others despise
Therefore it is near the eternal.

Tao Te Ching

Thought for the Day

'Fear grows out of the things we think, it lives in our own minds. Compassion grows out of the things we are, and lives in our hearts'.

Barbara Garrison

Water, water, water.

One of our biggest problems today is the fact that our vegetables are grown in ground that is drenched with fertilisers and pesticides and so devoid of minerals which are so very important for our well-being. Also, there is so much importation of fruit which is treated with preservatives to keep it alive until it arrives and also with pesticides and colourings.

There is a big increase in organic farming going back now to the time of my grandmothers farm.

Clematis Taken from Mary Lynne's & Einer's garden in Stavanger, Norway

Liver vessels –

Going into the liver :	The Hepatic Artery
	The Portal Vein
Leaving the liver :	The Hepatic Vein
	The Bile Duct

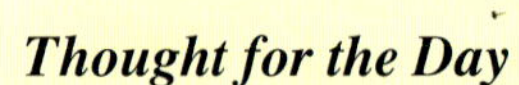

Thought for the Day

'If you bring forth what is inside you, what you bring forth will save you. If you don't bring forth what is inside you, what you don't bring forth will destroy you.'
Jesus

The Hepatic Artery

The Hepatic Artery is a large vessel. It carries pure blood to the liver from a connection to the abdominal aorta, which is a very large and very strong tube of muscle. If you lie down and put your fingers on a line down the middle of your abdomen below your chest bone, you should be able to feel the pulse of your blood being transported through your body.

The Portal Vein

The Portal Vein carries blood rich in nutrients which it has collected from what you have eaten and digested, which has already passed through the stomach, intestines and extracts the goodness from food you have eaten, plus the rubbish from junk food, soft drinks, alcohol, drugs and pain killers. As the saying goes, 'you are what you eat'.

This explains why people get liverish, sluggish, tired and irritable because everything is broken down in the liver and it holds on to the rubbish and eventually becomes very sad, so do you, because your liver governs how you feel in yourself.

The explanation for treatment and cleaning the liver follows.

The Bile Duct

The Bile Duct is a tiny little tube which carries bile, a bitter green liquid which is gathered from the liver cells and transports it to the digestive tract (duodenum) to aid in the digestion of your food.

Wild Violet

This little tube can become clogged with gravel from the Gall Bladder and this causes huge discomfort, pain, burping, indigestion and a feeling of being very sick with pain under the ribs on the right side and possibly going through to the back.

Reflexology: working on the acupuncture points on the feet give great relief and eases the problem in most cases, also it cleans out the liver provided medical checks are done.

The Hepatic Vein

The Hepatic Vein is a much smaller vessel than an artery. It arises from a passageway from the Hepatic Artery – much like a small side road off a main road. Its job is to take blood from the liver.

Thought for the Day

The way to use life is to do nothing through acting,
The way to use life is to do everything through being.
Lao-Tzu

The liver has two main lobes and is divided in itself into smaller lobes. The liver can become congested, but can clean itself out and regenerate its cells as has been proven by recent surgery techniques, when a small toddler was given a portion of her aunt's liver in a successful operation.

Diet to rest the Liver

Foods to avoid:

- Heavy fats
- Bacon, pork, ham, beef
- Eggs
- Cream, cheese
- Alcohol of all kinds
- No rich desserts
- No soft drinks

Foods allowed

- Fish (white), no smoked or oily fish
- Chicken, game
- Pasta, rice, millet
- Olive oil for cooking
- Plenty of vegetables and fruit
- A little potato
- Light milk, cultured yoghurt (organic)

Do not drink with meals, as this dilutes the digestive juices and interferes with proper digestion.

Alcohol should be avoided or taken very occasionally.

Herb tea or coffee may be taken twenty minutes before or after a meal.

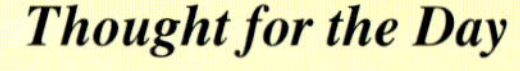

Thought for the Day

'A man's greatest strength develops at the point where he overcomes his greatest weakness.'

Eltier G. Letterman

No sugar or sugar products should be eaten except honey.

No white flour products should be eaten including puddings, ice cream, pastry, cakes.

No animal fats or very little including butter, cream, fatty meats, milk (except skimmed milk or goat's milk in small quantities) should be taken.

Camomile

Avoid soft drinks or chocolates.

Cherish your health; if it is good, preserve it. If it is unstable, improve it. If it is beyond what you can improve, get help.

Now we will talk about another very important organ.

The Pancreas

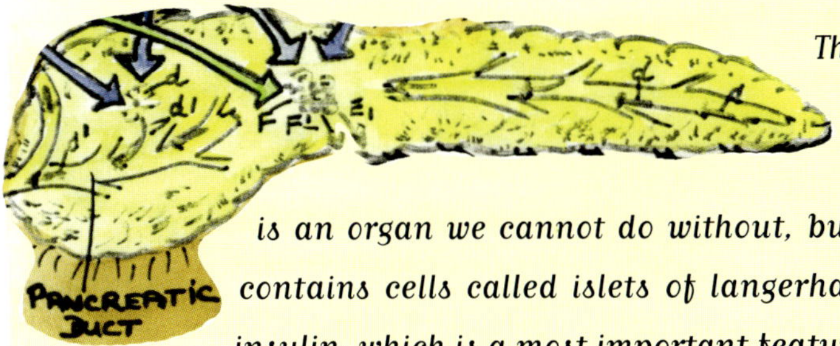

PANCREATIC DUCT

This very important organ lies tucked in behind the liver, gall bladder and stomach. It is an organ we cannot do without, but has a very complex job. It contains cells called islets of langerhans. Their job is to produce insulin, which is a most important feature in our blood sugar levels.

Through a duct which runs through it, it collects pancreatic juice and passes it into the intestine called the duodenum, which is the continuation of the stomach. Here its job is to help digest carbohydrates and break them down (carbohydrates are breads, cereals, pastas,

Thought for the Day

'A cloudy day is no match for a sunny disposition.'

William Arthur Ward

potatoes) these digested give us energy to keep going.

If it malfunctions and produces too little insulin, it causes a disease called diabetes which is becoming too common and is not confined to a specific age group, but is right across the board from young children right up to the elderly. It can be controlled by strict diet but in some cases it must be supported either by tablets or injections of insulin.

Wild Celery

Symptoms which need immediate attention:

- Constant thirst
- Too many visits to the toilet to pass urine
- Exhaustion
- Craving sweets
- Weight loss
- Boils or bad healing

A large number of people are living their life with sub-clinical diabetes, or diabetes which has not manifested itself to the extent that it is in need of control.

Foods to be permanently avoided:

1. Flour of all sorts: wheat, corn, rye and soy

2. All flour products: bread, toasts, cakes, pies, cookies, crackers, buns, doughnuts, spaghetti, macaroni, noodles and pizza. Allowed: spelt flour, rice flour, maize, millet and buckwheat.

3. Coffee, tea, cocoa, liquor, beer, wine, colas, carbonated beverages and soft drinks.

4. Sugars, candies, ice cream, artificial sweeteners.

5. Jellies, jams and marmalade.

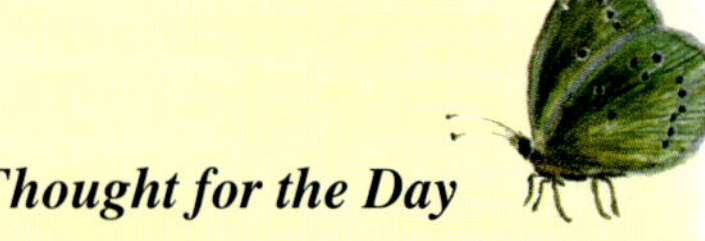

Thought for the Day

No day is without its duty, no duty without the strength to perform it.

6. Canned or processed foods.

7. Frozen fruits, strawberries, oranges and rhubarb.

8. Any food manufactured or adulterated by man, such as prepared breakfast cereal, or semi prepared like quick cook oatmeal.

Celery: counters acid formation in the blood and clears it out of the system.
Lemon: highly recommended (stewed in milk and taken as a diuretic).
Zinc, B vitamins and A & B.
Devils Claw- except for diabetics.
Nettles: excellent for circulation.

Honor the healer for his services
For the Lord created him
His skill comes from the Most High
And he is rewarded by kings.
The Healer's knowledge gives him standing
And wins him the admiration of the great.
The Lord has created medicines from the earth
And a sensible man will not disparage them.
Ecclesiasticus 38:1-4

To the lay mind it may be complicated by the theory that the 'the prime cause of cancer' is the replacement of the respiration of oxygen in normal body cells by a 'fermentation of sugar'. Dr. Otto Warburg

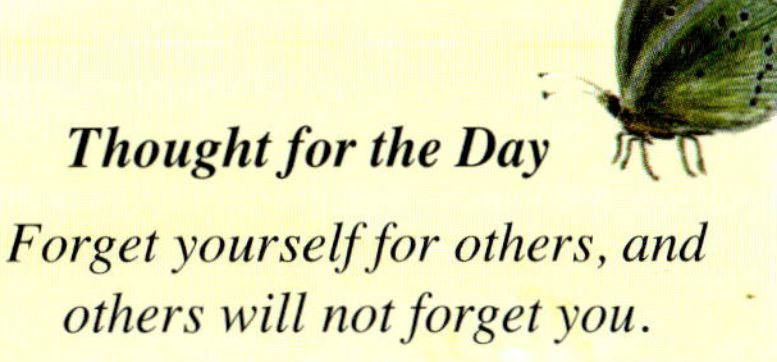

Thought for the Day

Forget yourself for others, and others will not forget you.

In today's world and modern diet, sedentary life style, processed food, overuse of sugar yeast and over use of antibiotics, the result is the huge increase in gut fermentation which causes lack of energy, exhaustion, bloating, offensive wind, leading to eventual chronic health problems. Dr. Warburg was right – babies are now being born with fermentation in their little gut, passed through the umbilical cord from mother, caused by:-

Fennel

1. *incorrect diet*
2. *too much hidden sugars*
3. *junk food*
4. *processed food*
5. *soft drinks and wine which is a fermented beverage.*
6. *over use of antibiotics causing breakdown of natural bacteria in the intestine. Yeast, breads, rolls, croissants, beer and wine contain yeast.*

Exercise, fresh air, change in diet habits, positive thinking, cutting down or cutting out stressful situations, daily bowel function, antioxidants, vitamins and minerals, sufficient intake of vitamin C, which is not retained in the body,

Thought for the Day

When you forgive,
remember to forget.

and is needed daily, particularly during stressful situations, and moderate drinking of alcohol.

7-8 glasses of water daily.

Red Clover

Signs from the body

- general exhaustion
- irritability
- get up and go – gone
- bowel movements changed – foul odour
- getting up during the night
- bloating after eating and wind
- loss of libido
- tired brain
- p.h. imbalance

take cider vinegar, super 8, anti parasitic

treatment:

regulation of body systems, Elimination of toxins, prolong life, quality of life.

The younger the patient the easier the cure.

New born babies are suffering from yeast because of mothers bad diet and over use of antibiotics and alcohol. The aim of treatment is to assist the body to heal itself – we cannot do without orthodox medicine.

Cancer (WDDTY Vol 18 No. 6 page 7)

Dr. Otto Warburg - a German Biochemist .

He was awarded two Nobel Prizes for medicine, but his work lay forgotten and discredited for many years. He died in 1970, but now it is being investigated again. Dr. Warburg, during his research in the 1930's,

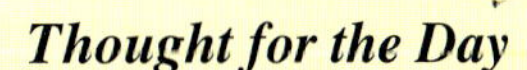

Don't grumble because you don't have what you want, be thankful you don't get what you deserve.

discovered that cancer did not need oxygen, but gained energy from **fermentation of sugar**, through a very detailed medical research with little to help him. In 1924, when there was very little cancer about, he proposed his theory, but it was not accepted. He died in 1970, but was true to his beliefs until then. However, now it is being investigated again, and Spanish researchers having investigated his theories, now say that there is 'strong support for Warburg hypothesis'.

Rosehip

Two radiologists at the University of Arizona have pointed out that they have been using the 'Warburg Effect' for years – in body scanning machines.

To the lay mind it may be complicated but the theory is that 'the Prime cause of cancer' is the replacement of the respiration of oxygen in normal body cells by a 'fermentation of sugar' Dr. Otto Warburg

Thought for the Day

I am done with great things and bit plans, great institutions and big success. I am for those tiny, invisible, loving human forces that work from individual to individual, creeping through the crannies of the world like so many rootlets, or like the capillary oozing water, which if given time will rend the hardest monuments of pride.

William James

The Urinary System

The Urinary System

The kidneys lie on either side of the rib cage between the ribs and the hip, tucked in almost under the protection of the lower ribs. They are the second most important organ in the body, in that their job is to take away toxic liquid waste, and therefore it is of prime importance that they are kept in good condition. This can be achieved by drinking plenty of water and having regular reflexology treatments to keep the kidneys free of toxins. I am not going to go into medical details about the structure of the kidneys because it is too detailed, but an excellent reference book is 'A Pictorial Handbook of Anatomy and Physiology' by Dr. James Bevan.

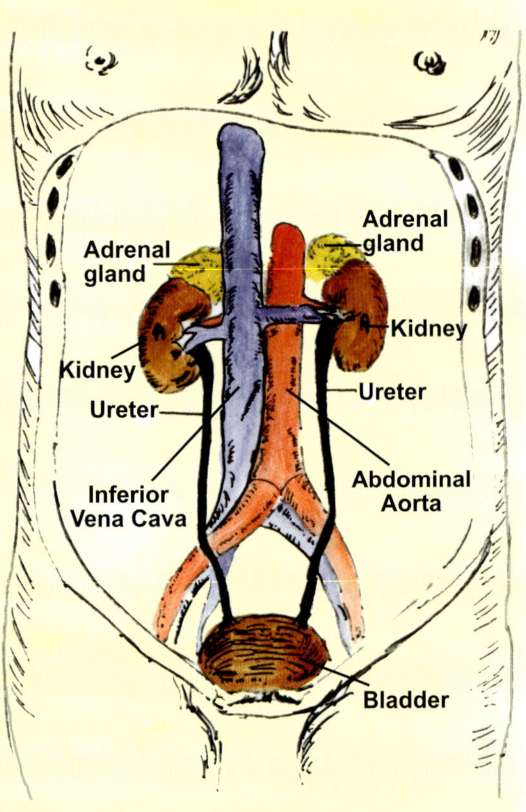

The diseases that affect the kidneys are nephritis, Urethritis, Cystitis, and Uraemia.

Uraemia is caused by damage to one or both kidneys and necessitates dialysis and possibly kidney transplant.

Itis is inflammation. Cystitis is a very uncomfortable inflammation in the urinary tract which causes severe pain on excretion of urine, and the constant feeling of the need to pass urine when there is nothing there. It is, however, treatable.

cranberry

Thought for the Day

Our greatest experiences are our quieter moments.

Nietzsche (1844-1900)

Urethritis is another inflammatory process involving the urinary tract which can cause severe back ache and stinging, and left untreated can be the cause of an individual becoming seriously sick.

All symptoms relating to kidney infection need medical treatment with antibiotics. Because of the importance of the organ, pain across the back, discomfort passing urine or signs of blood in the urine should never be left untreated or ignored.

Thought for the Day

The miracle comes quietly into
the mind that stops an instant
and is still.
From a Course in Miracles

Reproductive System

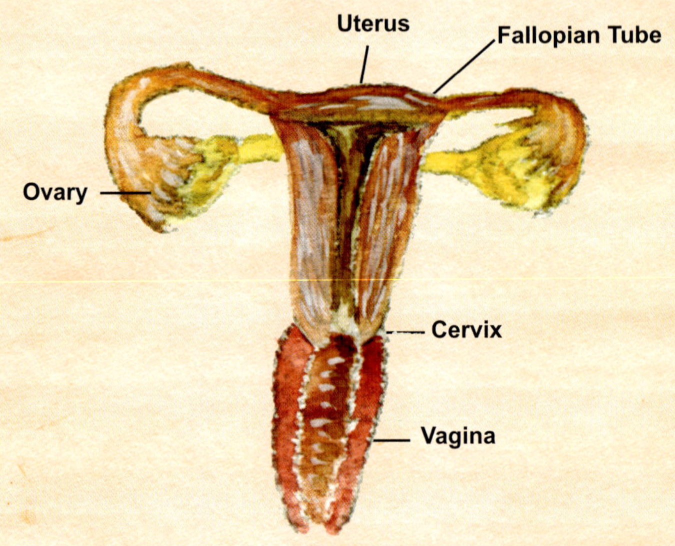

The Cell

The basic unit of life. All cells develop from one basic cell – the fertilized ovum.

Each cell is surrounded by pliable and protective membrane, through which substances pass both ways. In the centre is the nucleus, which controls the cells activities. Chromosomes carry the genes that determine the cells activities.

Evening Primrose

Each cell requires different substances, obtained from the circulation, fats, carbohydrates, amino acids and various salts.

Female reproductive system

The female reproductive system, which comes under the Endocrine system, is a very complex area to cover, so we will briefly cover problems

Thought for the Day

The quieter you become,
the more you hear.
Baba Ram Dass

with periods and PMS which are the main areas of trouble.

Thought for the Day

Complete possession is proved only by giving, all you are unable to give possesses you.

Andre Gide

PMS, or premenstrual tension can be caused by various disturbances in metabolism and endometriosis in the body, which also embeds itself in and around the womb, causing a blockage of energy and therefore pain and pressure, resulting in mental stress, also known as PMT. (Refer to picture of fungus in digestive chapter)

Star Flower

These problems can be dealt with and cleared in a matter of weeks by a yeast free diet and special natural remedies which can be taken and which help to clear out from top to toe. Also recommended – reflexology and acupuncture.

Male reproductive system

Most important for men over 50 years is to have their GP do a blood test for PSA levels, which show changes in their reproductive area, necessitating attention. This is a test for the prostate and shows if there are changes.

Saw Palmetto

Vitus Agnus Castus

The Endocrine System

The Endocrine System

A very complex system.

Pineal, Pituitary, Parathyroid, Thyroid, Hypothalamus, Thymus, Adrenal Gland, Pancreas and reproductive system.

Ductless structures whose secretions pass directly into the circulation, hormones influence the activity of specific target tissues elsewhere in the body. Pituitary is the governing gland; it controls the thyroid, adrenal cortex and glands.

The hypothalamic gland has a controlling influence in growth, sexual activity, thyroid function, lactation, water balance, carbohydrate, protein and fat metabolism.

The Parathyroid , 4 in number embedded posterior thyroid, regulate plasma, calcium and phosphorus levels.

The Pituitary, between the eyes, behind the nose, master gland, produces seven hormones.

Refer to Dr. James Bevan for reading, or Dorling Kindersley do a very good book on anatomy and physiology.

Lavender

Camomile

Thought for the Day

If you can give but one gift, make it the gift of good example.

The Skin

The Skin

The skin comes under accessory organs and depending on the size of the body it covers from little to large, it is huge and very, very important – it covers and protects, it is important in helping to regulate body temperature and as you know comes in all shades from pale to very black, depending on the country.

Marigold

I remember being fascinated at school drawing a sketch of the layers of skin and its contents, epidermis and dermis, microscopic blood vessels, nerves, sweat glands called salacious glands, hair follicles, subcutaneous tissue or fatty tissue. The top layer is actually dead cells which flake off and are replaced by continuous growth.

Here is my effort at repeating the drawing I did years ago.

Thought for the Day
'Men dig their own graves with their teeth'.

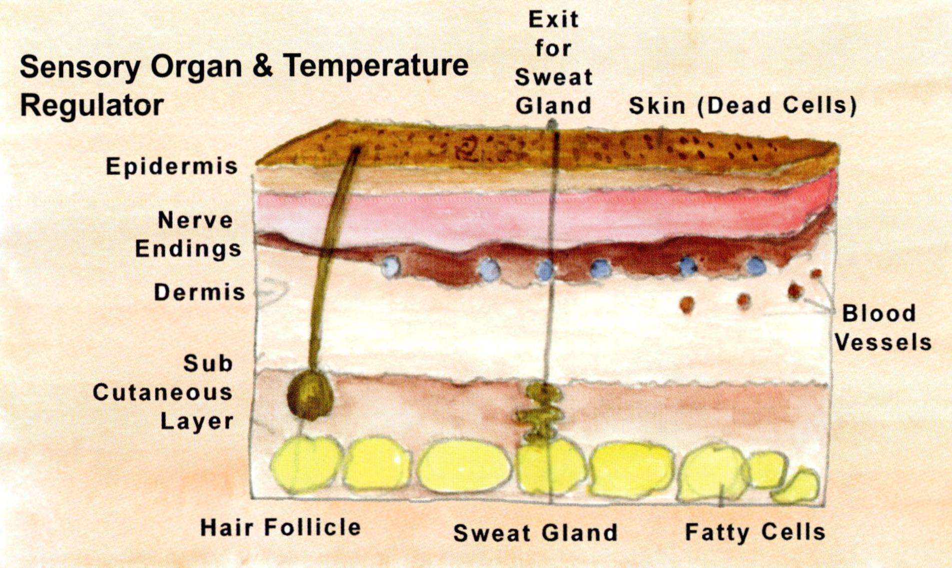

The malpagian layer is the one which gives dark people their skin colour.

The average body temperature taken under the arm should read an average 96.4F or 36.8C.

The skin is helped by being regularly brushed to get rid of dead tissues plus a healthy intake of water. No need to go into great medical detail here. It's too complicated, but a simple synopsis might I hope give you a greater understanding of the package.

Parsley

The skin and the condition it's in shows an experienced eye the condition of the body inside because in cases of a toxic body what is inside will break out on the skin in the form of spots, acne, rashes, an irritating itch which cannot be seen, but is usually indicative of an underlying fungal infection, or ulcers on the lower limbs where circulation is impaired.

1. **the Epidermis** or top layer of skin is where this occurs
2. **the Dermis**, which is underneath the top layer, has nerves, glands, blood vessels and hair follicles.

Evening Primrose

The **Subcutaneous** tissue or adipose tissue is fatty and contains nerves and blood vessels.

Psoriasis

Psoriasis is a chronic skin complaint that causes a great deal of distress among its sufferers. It is characterised by the occurrence of dry, reddish patches on the skin which are covered with silvery white scales. The parts of the body most commonly affected are the elbows, knees, scalp, nails and in the most severe cases almost the whole of

Thought for the Day

'Man who drinks medicine but eats badly wastes his knowledge'.

the skin may be involved. The young adult appears to be the most susceptible, although it can develop much later in life. It represents about four percent of all skin diseases, and estimates from the U.S. puts the figure around 7 – 8 million, which would be about 2% of the whole population, making it an unsolved medical problem of considerable proportions.

Nettle

In the early years of the nineteenth century an observant medical man was able to put the complaint in its proper perspective and confirm too that it was not contagious. To the patient it is a most distressing anti-social disease, for which there only appears to be temporary relief. The good news is that there is a natural remedy which not only clears young psoriasis completely but with persistence, psoriasis of long standing can be relieved too and kept at bay.

Detoxing for a month with yeast free and dairy free diet, on correct diet psoriasis will start to reduce in anger and can be controlled very well, once trigger foods are found.

I do hope that you will now have a good look at and appreciate the miracle of divine engineering which you are walking around in, and which keeps you upright, mobile, but which you must look after and treat it, and the YOU whom it encases, with respect and loving care.

PAINTED BY Niamh Moran aged 15

Thought for the Day

The best thing to spend on your children is your time.

Stress

Stress

'Stress is the non-specific response of the body to any demand'.

Apart from the cycle of physical development that is obvious to everybody, there are cycles of spiritual and of soul development.

The purpose of life is to pass through all these cycles with increasing awareness, living them through so that in the course of life the whole potential of the Higher Self may be realised. Anything that will assist this process of conscious realisation, even events that initially may appear negative, is considered positive. Anything that darkens consciousness is negative and will sooner or later lead to illness.

Star of Bethlehem

The key issue in this psychodynamic approach is consciously to aim for and accept constructive change.

The Tibetan Master DJWal Kul taught that there is a direct link between man's unconscious and the plant kingdom, man is therefore able to contact his own essential nature of Higher Self at an unconscious level through plant nature and so restore harmony within himself.

For example, walk into a perfumed rose garden on a fine day and become aware mentally what is happening to you. Communing with nature, a total relaxation takes place within a very short time, bringing about the relaxing of the higher mind, releases stress and enhances the ability of the mind to relate to the glory of nature.

Thought for the Day

Sister in deep silence, be still and open your mind,
Sink deep into the peace that awaits for you beyond
the frantic, riotous thoughts and sights and sounds of
this insane world.
From A Course in Miracles

Rose Hip - Vit. C

Clematis

Stress is one of the results of our prosperity. Chronic stress is the major health problem of modern society. We are victims of our own technology. None of us wants to give up the most luxurious style of living that man has ever known. We don't want to turn back the clock and give up modern conveniences such as fast cars and 'planes that can whisk us to our destination in a matter of hours.

Andrew Slevin age 10

Excessive stress has been linked to many different kinds of illness from low back pain to cancer.

Impatiens

Research is showing with increasing regularity that stress is associated with increased susceptibility to illness in general.

The function of physical illness is that of final corrective. It is a final warning light, indicating that something must be done or total failure will follow.

It is the way the body handles the stress which is of the utmost importance. The same body has a stereotyped biochemical response to demands whether pleasant or unpleasant. The types of stress may be different but they all elicit the same biological response.

Some of us can stand more stress than others because we are made of tougher 'material' or have been strengthened over the years to certain kinds of stresses. As long as we experience stress within our own elastic limits, we probably won't have any ill effects from it.

Thought for the Day

If you can spend a perfectly useless afternoon in a perfectly useless manner, you have learned how to live.

Lin Yutang (1895-1976)

If we are stressed beyond our limit without sharing the cause with someone, trouble lies on the horizon. If it continues far beyond our stress threshold we experience a complete nervous breakdown.

Many individuals carry an amazing level of stress without obvious side effects; on the other hand a more 'timid' individual would succumb to a lower level.

A complete breakdown situation is reached when the stress threshold is pushed to the limit. There are pleasant and unpleasant stresses :

Rock Rose

- High levels of noise and lack of stimulation
- Knowing your stress
- Coping with same
- Boredom
- Frustrated ambition
- Conflict
- Exorbitant work demands
- Time pressure
- Bullying
- Suppressed emotions
- Midlife crisis
- Financial problems

Thought for the Day

Don't worry, don't hurry,
you're only here for a short visit,
so be sure to stop and
smell the flowers.
Walter Hagen

According to Dr Harry Johnson, fatigue is often emotional in origin and is related to boredom.

If you are suffering from extreme boredom you are likely to start work in the morning feeling bad and not having any energy for your work, no interest because it presents no challenge. More rest is not the answer; a complete review of the work scene is called for. The very serious psychological damage done to people by

being told –

'At your age learn to live with it'.

'What do you expect?'

'I cannot help you'.

These statements set in a depression which in turn affects the whole, mind, body, spirit. Whereas every single person has the power within them to keep themselves well and if ill or in disharmony with themselves, the ability to persuade their bodies back to a healthy, happy situation. It takes discipline though. I have at this time seen many adults and children come through this, some with resentment initially, but with joy in their hearts when the balance is achieved. Then they know themselves 'you are what you eat', plus mentally and emotional harmony are an important factor which cannot be forgotten.

Cherry Plum

Hugs

It's wondrous what a hug can do,
A hug can cheer you when you're blue,
A hug can say 'I love you so'
Or 'Gee, I hate to see you go'.

A hug is 'Welcome back again'
And 'Great to see you' or 'Where have you been?'
A hug can soothe a small child's pain
And bring a rainbow after rain.

The Hug! There's just no doubt about it,
We scarcely could survive without it.
A hug delights and warms and charms.
It must be why God gave us arms.

Thought for the Day

'Disease is an end product - a physical manifestation of a negative state of mind'.
Wm. Edward Bach

Hugs are great for Fathers and Mothers,
Sweet for Sisters, swell for Brothers,
And chances are some favourite Aunts
Love them more than potted plants.

Kittens crave them, puppies love them,
Heads of State are not above them.
A hug can break the language barrier
And make the dullest day seem merrier.

No need to fret about the store of them
The more you give, the more there are of them.
So stretch those arms without delay
And give someone a hug today.

My friend Audrey Carney gave me this years ago
(Author Unknown)

Thought for the Day

'Good friends are good for your health'.
Irwan Sardson

Lavender

Human life, man on this planet is but a greater concept of creation. We live within a wider frame of reference, a more comprehensive unity, more or less like a cell within a human body.

Every person is one of two things, a unique individual and a vital and essential part of the greater unity, the greater whole. The development of every individual human being follows a programmed course of action and reaction. Every human being has a mission, task, destiny, karma or whatever we may call it. Each has the unconscious desire to live in harmony.

When the personality is not in harmony with its soul there is disruption, congestion, friction, disharmony and loss of energy. These conditions are first present in subtle, non-material ways but progress to the material level manifesting first in negative moods and later in physical illness.

Dr. Edward Bach said disease is caused by two basic errors:

1. The Personality is not acting in accord with the soul. Health exists when the mind and body are functioning in harmony and illness besets us when stress upsets this balance.
2. In all separate areas where personality has turned away from love and virtue, positive character traits become distorted and this leads to negative soul states and moods.

This anonymous quotation puts it perfectly:

"Righteousness without love makes us hard,
Faith without love makes us fanatical,
Power without love makes us brutal,
Orderliness without love makes us petty".

Thought for the Day

'If there is kindness I can show or any good thing I can do to any fellow being, let me do it now, and not defer or neglect it, as I shall not pass this way again'.

William Penn

Stress comes in two forms. The various pressures or demands from the external environment, which could stem from family, job, friends are called external stress. Internal stress is caused by pressure you put on yourself by being ambitious, competitive and aggressive. In most cases these internal stresses have far more harmful effects than do external.

Mind

Body

Spirit

Stress

Disharmony

Dis-ease

Breakdown

Chronic illness

Camomile

Stress – the biggest factor – affects the mind. This causes psychosomatic illness which in turn affects the organs which are sensitive and have feelings of their own, just think of your stomach – the way it tightens before a big event.

Resistance, Repair and Recovery

Thought for the Day

'The less medication a body has the higher it stands in virtue'.
Parccelecus

The root of all illness is poison through imbalance. Holistic treatment is based on the theory that disturbance of the parts diseases the whole, so what natural healing requires is a treatment for the whole body – or the whole person.

One of the most increasing areas of holistic therapy is the use of essential oils. The healing powers of aromatherapy are fast being recognised. It is widely practised in France by the medical profession, and there too one must be a qualified medic to practice. Although 5000 years old, the use of essential oils fell from grace with the introduction of modern medicine.

These oils work with the forces of nature and not against them and therefore bring about true healing, making a comeback with astonishing force. In his many books Professor Sevan Binet (a former Dean of the Faculty of Medicine in Paris) as written by Dr. Jean Valnet has commented time and again about the extraordinary healing properties of substances found in plants. The names of the most eminent researchers, doctors, biologists and pharmacists continually appear among the authors of the numerous works that deal with plants and essential oils.

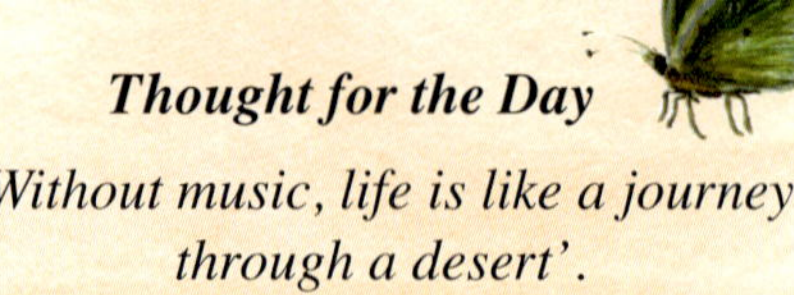

Thought for the Day

'Without music, life is like a journey through a desert'.
Pat Conroy

Vervain

What are essential oils?

They are treasures of nature from time immemorial, the tiny droplets from plants, flowers and trees which can be used as mouth washes, gargles, baths, foot baths, compresses, but most commonly by the caring hands on treatments of aromatherapy massage, by which means the essential oils are massaged into the skin or part of the whole body, depending on the problem being treated.

This Instant

Perhaps this very instant is your time. Your own, your peculiar, your promised and presaged moments, out of all moments forever.

This very instant – that is all we have,
We make plans for the future, we invoke memories of the past,
But really, all we have to deal with and to act in is the moment at hand.

Fenugreek

We cannot stop its going,
We cannot hurry the next moment on its way.
Like everyone else in the world we're partners in the dull, humdrum,
Dazzling, fabulous, totally unpredictable moment.

And if we have a time that is 'our time', its right
now.
It has to be, because there isn't any other.
Maybe we've had times in the past that were
special for us'
Maybe the future will hold precious moments.
But the only time that is truly 'our time' is this
time,
Where we are, right now,
And what we do with this time is ours to decide.

'Each moment is mine, to make as beautiful or as painful as I choose'.

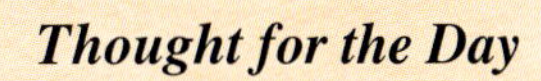

Thought for the Day

When you turn green with envy
you are ripe for trouble.

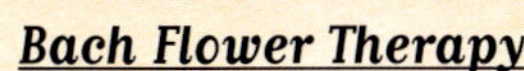

Bach Flower Therapy

'Heal thyself' is at the very heart of Dr. Edward Bach, the great Harley St. physician who discovered the 'Flower Remedies' and gave up his lucrative practice to dedicate the remainder of his short life to the discovery of 'healing by means of wild flowers, shrubs and water'.

Feverfew

The aim of a particular life is for the Higher Self to bring the intentions of the soul to realisation in the personality. Disease is, according to the interpretation, disharmony or distortion of frequencies within or between different levels of the aura and the Higher Self.

The information pattern of this distortion shows itself at the first etheric level, which manifests at different areas of the physical body, and then takes months, indeed even years before it manifests itself as a disease in some area of the human body. Flowers contain the same natural energy and life force as people. (Plants suffer from the shock of a move, or being ignored, their life force disappears). - Collapsed with no energy, no water.

Our soul can be crushed by psychological damage, which in turn causes physical illness.

To make it easy – what goes on in your head affects your body, e.g. if you are in a situation where you are constantly ostracised you feel resentful, suppressed, wronged. If you do not do something to ease this your system will fill with bitterness and anger and you will become ill.

*An old Chinese medicine man says:
Not WHAT is wrong with you
But WHO is wrong with you.*

This speaks volumes – it tells us we are not a person of free will but perhaps bullied, controlled and suppressed by our peer – in other words our 'free will' is not free.

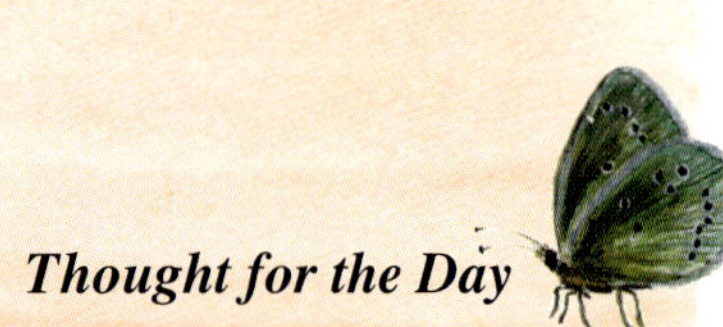
Thought for the Day

Accept that some days you are the pigeon and some days you are the statue (think about it).

Roger C. Anderson

One of my hobbies over the years has been collecting 'quips', poems, and 'sayings'. One of these comes to mind – 'what a child grows up with'.

Children learn what they live

If children live with criticism they learn to condemn.
If children live with hostility they learn to fight.
If children live with ridicule they learn to be shy.
If children live with shame they learn to feel guilty.

If children live with tolerance they learn to be patient.
If children live with encouragement they learn confidence.

If children live with praise they learn to appreciate.
If children live with fairness they learn justice.

If children live with security they learn to have faith.
If children live with approval they learn to like themselves.

If children live with acceptance and friendship they learn to find love in the world.

And remember these children grow into Adults.

Thought for the Day

One of the best things about the future is that it comes one day at a time.

Faith in things we cannot see requires a child's simplicity.
O Father grant once more to me a simple childlike faith again.
Helen Steiner Rice

It is so true, if a young character is not strong enough he or she will succumb to sarcasms and hints thrown constantly by an adult who has not resolved a chip on their shoulder, or an inner trauma which causes deep unhappiness.

As children we respond to love and a certain amount of discipline to guide our character – then we grow strong in love and understanding and so feel cherished – from this a beautiful grounded adult will bloom who will in turn hand on to others what he has gained.

We also learn through hurt, violation and loneliness and if this is dealt with properly, the result is a strong and psychologically happy human.

Insight

It is not only children who dissolve under chastisement, or the 'why are you not as good as....', 'shut up – get out and play', 'eat your dinner or else'. It's parents venting their own anger on the little ones.

Adults too are at both ends of this tirade of abuse at home and in the work place.

The people who dish out this abuse should look into themselves and try and sort out the reason for their 'abusive chip'.

Thought for the Day

Countless unseen details are often the only difference between mediocre and magnificent.

Our parents

Erin May Ross

Our parents cast long shadows over our lives. When we grow up we imagine that we can walk into the sun, free of them. We don't realise until its too late that we have no choice in the matter they're always ahead of us.

We carry them within us all our lives, in the shape of our face, the way we walk, the sound of our voice, our skin, our hair, our hands, our heart. We try all our lives to separate ourselves from them and only when they are dead do we find we are indivisible.

We grow to expect that our parents, like the weather, will always be with us. Then they go, leaving a mark like a handprint on glass or a wet kiss on a rainy day, and with their death we are no longer children.

Richard Eyre

Thought for the Day

If you are through changing,
your all through.

Dance like no one is watching.

We convince ourselves that life will be better after we get married, have a baby and then another. Then we are frustrated that the kids aren't old enough and we'll be more content when they are. After that we're frustrated that we have teenagers to deal with. We will certainly be happy when they are out of that stage. We tell ourselves that our life will be complete when our spouse gets a better job, when we can afford a nicer car, are able to go on a nice holiday, or when we retire.

The truth is, there's no better time to be happy than right now. Your life will always be filled with challenges. It's best to admit this to yourself and decide to be happy anyway. Alfred D. Souza once said, 'For a long time it had seemed to me that life was about to begin – real life. But there was always some obstacle in the way, something to be gotten through first, some unfinished business, time still to be served, a debt to be paid. Then life would begin. At last it dawned on me that these obstacles were my life'.

This perspective has helped me see that there is no way to happiness. Happiness is the way. So treasure every moment that you have. And treasure it more because you shared it with someone special, special enough to spend your time with and remember that time waits for no one…so stop waiting until you finish school, until you go back to school, until you lose ten pounds, until you have kids, until your kids leave the house, until you start work, until you retire, until you get married, until you move, until Friday night, until Sunday morning, until you get a new car or home, until your car or home is paid off, until Spring, until Summer, until Autumn, until Winter, until the first or fifteenth, until your song comes on, until someone calls you until you die – to decide there is no better time than now to be happy.

Thought for the Day

Happiness is a journey, not a destination. *Love reduces friction to a fraction*

Eleanor Roosevelt wrote:

Many people will walk in and out of your life,
But only true friends will leave footprints in your heart.

To handle yourself, use your head,
To handle others, use your heart.
Anger is only one letter short of danger.

If someone betrays you once it is his fault,
If he betrays you twice, it is yours.

Great minds discuss ideas,
Average minds discuss events,
Small minds discuss people.

He who loses money, loses much.
He who loses a friend loses much more.
He who loses faith loses all.

Beautiful young people are accidents of nature,
But Beautiful old people are works of art.
Learn from the mistakes of others,
You can't live long enough to make them all yourself.

Friends, you and me ...you brought another friend... and then there were three. We started our group...our circle of friends...and like that circle...there is no beginning or end.

Yesterday is history, tomorrow is a mystery,
today is a gift.
That is why we call it the present.!!!

Thought for the Day

Your work is to discover your work
and then with all your heart give
yourself to it
Buddha

Complimentary Medicine

Complimentary Medicine

A wonderful message from George Carlin

The paradox of our time in history is that we have taller buildings but shorter tempers, wider freeways but narrower viewpoints. We spend more, but have less; we buy more, but enjoy less. We have bigger houses and smaller families; more conveniences but less time. We have more degrees but less sense, more knowledge, but less judgement, more experts, yet more problems, more medicine, but less wellness.

Thought for the Day

Words break no bones
but they do break hearts.

We drink too much, smoke too much, spend too recklessly, laugh too little, drive too fast, get too angry, stay up too late, get up too tired, read too little, watch TV too much, and pray too seldom. We have multiplied our possessions but reduced our values. We talk too much, love too seldom and hate too often.

We have learned to make a living but not a life. We've added years to life but not life to years. We've been all the way to the moon and back, but have trouble crossing the street to meet a new neighbour. We conquered outer space but not inner space. We've done larger things, but not better things.

We've cleaned up the air, but polluted the soul. We've conquered the atom, but not our prejudice. We write more, but learn less. We plan more, but accomplish less. We've learned to rush, but not to wait. We build more computers to hold more information, to produce more copies than ever, but we communicate less and less.

Vervain

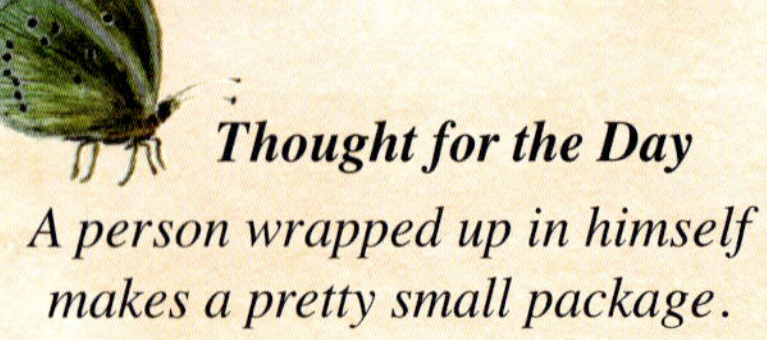

Thought for the Day

A person wrapped up in himself makes a pretty small package.

These are the times of fast food and slow digestion, big men and small character, steep profits and shallow relationships. These are the days of two incomes but more divorce, fancier houses but broken homes. These are the days of quick trips, disposable diapers, throwaway morality, one night stands, overweight bodies, and pills to do everything from cheer, to quiet, to kill. It is a time when there is much in the showroom window and nothing in the stockroom. A time when technology can bring this letter to you and a time when you can choose to share this insight or just hit delete.

Life is not measured by the number of breaths we take, but by the moments that take our breath away.

How to stay young

1. *Throw out nonessential numbers. This includes age, weight and height. Let the doctor worry about them. That is why you pay him/her.*

2. *Keep only cheerful friends. The grouches pull you down.*

3. *Keep learning. Learn more about the computer, crafts, gardening, whatever. Never let the brain idle. 'An idle mind is the devil's workshop'. And the devil's name is Alzheimers.*

4. *Enjoy the simple things.*

5. *Laugh often, long and loud. Laugh until you gasp for breath.*

Viola

6. *The tears happen. Endure, grieve, and move on. The only person who is with us our entire life is ourselves. Be ALIVE while you are alive.*

7. *Surround yourself with what you love, whether its family, pets, keepsakes, music, plants, hobbies, whatever. Your home is your refuge.*
8. *Cherish your health; if it is good, preserve it. If it is unstable, improve it. If it is beyond what you can improve, get help.*

9. *Don't take guilt trips. Take a trip to the mall, to the next county, to a foreign country, but do not go to where the guilt is.*

10. *Tell people you love that you love them at every opportunity.*

Crategus

The primary goal of complimentary medicine is to strengthen the patients' bodily functions so that they may follow their natural course and rid the body of whatever bacteria, virus or inflammation is present. When we use antibiotics which rid the body of infection we can never be too sure that they do not 'kill off' the valuable bacteria which are very necessary for maintaining good health in our intestines in the first place.

All health problems stem from an imbalance in the system but most likely in the intestine – Asthma for instance, a major problem in young children- can be caused by food. Changing those foods and treating the imbalance restores the harmony.

Thought for the Day

Forget the faults of others by remembering your own.

Evidence of this can be seen in the number of children and young adults who have been treated successfully, but asthma too can be caused by environmental stress and pollutants.

Hippocrates *(47-360 BC) was the Father of Alternative Medicine. He taught men to treat the whole physical condition, to treat the whole personality, not just a few symptoms, to examine not just the man, but the life and habits, but above all to treat for the latent capacity of the human body to heal itself.*

Nature is a wonderful thing, and the closer we adhere to its healing ways the more harmony we can bring to a failing constitution and to restore this harmony is to give a new lease of life.

In order to gain harmony and balance in our stressful lives and to attain the ultimate in good health – these are examples of how complimentary medicine helps:-
By ridding the body of toxic waste which gathers in the organs and causes discomfort- be it digestive or fluid retention, indicating in itself an underlying problem. Knowing how to cope with this a trained therapist will decide which area of complimentary medicine or a combination of more than one will be used. Usually reflexology and nutritional guidance.

Bergamot

Thought for the Day

Live simply so others may simply live.

Reflexology

Thought for the Day

Much happiness is overlooked because it costs nothing.

Reflexology is based on the theory that every organ in the body has a corresponding point or zone in the feet or hands through which by a gentle pressure massage the body's ability to heal itself comes into its own.

Zone therapy as it was originally known works on the energy channels in the body. Its result must be seen to be believed, and the healing process which the body goes through may cause a little discomfort while cleaning out, but the result is a new lease of life, therefore a zest for living.

What can I say except that there is nothing like it. It's at the top of the list where treatment is concerned. When God made man he put all the nerve endings to all parts of the body in the soles of the feet and palms of the hands. At least 5,000 years old, it was practised long before orthodox medicine came into being and carvings in Egypt show the slave sitting cross-legged with his master sitting behind him, with his foot alongside the slaves hip level where he was massaging the 'boss's' foot.

Reflex zone therapy is not only relaxing, it brings relief to every part of the body by cleaning the organs of toxic waste which is then removed from the body by the kidneys, the bowel, the skin (by sweat) and the lungs.

Amazing reactions occur followed by a great and rewarding healing within, plus a feeling of lightness and well being and returned energy. A moderate exclusion diet undertaken during the course of treatment is of great benefit.

Thought for the Day

'Love a little, trust often, but always paddle your own canoe.

Given to me by my wonderful nephew Joseph

It just makes you feel so darn good. But having said this, while undergoing treatment your body plays funny little tricks – depending how toxic your system is you will not feel well overnight, you must go through the downs before the ups.

Everyone reacts differently, so one can never say it is going to be A, B or C. Its not, it could be X,Y, or Z. So observe and go along with it and drink plenty of warm water. You will never look back and a treatment every couple of weeks will keep you on your toes.

Acupuncture

One of the most highly respected areas of Ancient medicine is Acupuncture.

It is thousands of years old, and dates back to thousands of years before western medicine came into being. It was used in China for centuries with Chinese herbs, its aim being to unblock the energy channels in the body, and therefore correct balance.

I highly recommend acupuncture as a treatment for many illnesses, with tremendous wellbeing the result.

Discipline and meditation

Discipline is essential for mind and body.

You must create a discipline for your self. Do not allow your body or your mind continual freedom.

It's a case of setting up a task every day, and doing that task, be it meditation, reading, painting or whatever, but it's your time, your space, under your control. It's difficult at first but it becomes a habit and a very good one for mental harmony.

Start with short meditation morning and evening. Start with just shutting down for ten minutes at a time just to find stillness.

Discipline too is doing the task which must be done, and which you least wish to do. Do it first and do it well – and see how good you feel – remember – as you sow so shall you reap.

Meditation – switching everything off – listening to your inner self.

It is the responsibility of each of us to:

1. To find out who WE are.
2. Why we are here.
3. Where we are going.

We are all unique. If you find that you don't fit with your compatriots – go out and find yourself. Only you can do it.

As Oscar Wilde said, 'The true perfection of man lies, not in what man has, but in what man is'.

Thought for the Day

The heart already knows what the mind can only dream of.

1. Not to allow ourselves to be influenced by others, but to go INSIDE and find our real selves, and act on that.
2. We are all on earth for a purpose and to achieve our very best with whatever we set out to be or do. And remember – give something back – its called 'Tithing' your earnings – in other words, what the universe gives you – return a FRACTION- it will multiply a hundredfold.

The nice thing about meditation is that it makes sense – it makes 'doing nothing' quite respectable!

This form of meditation and self healing is of primary importance in the re-establishing of wellness in mind and body.

It just means 'having your own space', finding time to shut down your mind (and your mind will slow down your body) from the stresses of everyday life taking ten minutes – twenty- half hour or hour to unwind and listen to your inner self.

Decide where you want to be -at home or away from home or at the sea if you are close by – there is nothing as wonderful as listening to the sea - closing your eyes and getting away from everybody and everything. Not only can it make you feel better but you also cope better with life in general, particularly if you are in a stressful situation at home or in your workplace.

Life is in general so stressful these days – it's a battle for survival – work is harder – more technical – modern technology has brought its own

Thought for the Day

Trust your heart.

problems – geopathic waves, radiation, fumes, phones.

Thought for the Day
Yesterday is but a dream,
tomorrow is a vision of hope.

And guess what? 'all invented by man'. God in his creation gave us brains and ability but in the rush to achieve and perform have we gone overboard? Look at what is happening with the ozone layer for instance – but we just don't want to listen – more cars, more fumes, more phones, computers, it's frightening but when will it stop, or what can <u>**YOU**</u> do to ease it?

<u>**Health by suggestion**</u>

It is impossible to estimate to what extent the mind influences the body.

Fear, anxiety and worry have a detrimental effect on the health. It is only logical to assume therefore that thoughts of happiness, faith and love will have a beneficial effect on the body.

Think health and you will achieve health.

It is stern self-discipline, that is at the base of all good health.

'If evil comes not, then our fears are vain, and if they do, fear but augments the pain' Sir T. Moore

Herbal Medicine

When used properly and with care and wisdom, herbs are provided to keep your body well.

The tonic our grannies used every spring was nettles – gathered, stewed and made into a brew to spring clean the system and protect it from illness. Unfortunately, this is not

done now, but why not start again. After all, they are free like all the other herbs which are growing and not even noticed except by the animals – even our dogs and cats – watch them – they go for couch grass if they have an upset stomach and they clean themselves out, where you go for an antibiotic – they return to nature.

Thought for the Day
Look to this day, for it is life.

Also for good reading 'Healing Herbs in Ireland' by Paula Regan – a lovely book – very easy reading and from her you might be convinced to start your own herb garden at home, remember no side effects, used properly.

Many herbs have anti-viral effect. Lemon, sage and thyme being three of the well known ones. Others are rosemary, clove, oregano, peppermint.

Self-heal, another herb, well accounted for in the herbal books, has the ability to kill the herpes virus, applied topically.

A large number of essential oils too are antiviral, anti inflammatory, antibiotic and antibacterial but always make sure they are pure and never take internally. Read a good book on how to apply. 'The Fragrant Pharmacy' is a recommended read, also Danielle Ryman, Shirley Price, the original devotees of aromatherapy.

How to heal yourself

Now, my friends, it is time to know how to heal yourselves. All I have ever done is give advice and shown you where you are hurting and where the disharmony is – you have made yourselves well by following a little discipline and allowed your body time to heal itself.

Rosemary

Often it means breaking down defences i.e. my old one 'I'm not suffering from stress'. I'm just breaking up from emotional and physical exhaustion but my mind will not let me stop, because until I enter my mind and look inside myself for the reason for the stress, my mind is in control and driving me to the brink of 'burn out'.

So stop! Look inside and listen to who you are, why you are here and what is your purpose. Sometimes it takes a breakdown to say STOP!.

Herbs to use at home

Green tea

Parts used : the buds and leaves.

Indications : Toning the system, diuretic, helps in de-toxing, taken as tea or capsules.

Papaya

Parts used : Leaf

Indications : acts as digestive enzyme, helps liver and pancreas.

Sage

Meadow Sweet

Parts used: Flowering tips.

Indications Oedema, rheumatism, colds and flu.

Butchers Broom

Parts used: Root

Indications: circulation problems, varicose veins, congestion and haemorrhoids.

Thought for the Day

Today people know the price of everything and the value of nothing.

Witch Hazel

Parts used: Leaf

Indications: varicose veins, weak capillaries, also used for cosmetic lotion.

Artichoke

Parts used: leaf

Indications: Digestive, liver and gall bladder problems, constipation.

Boldo

Parts used: leaf

Indication : digestive and gall bladder – sluggish liver.

Charcoal

Indications : gastro intestinal – wind – bloating

Hawthorn

Parts used: flowering tips

Indications: nervousness, anxiety, heart problems.

Valerian

Parts used: Roots

Indications: sedative – insomnia

Dandelion

Parts used: Root

Indications: liver cleansing, relieves small gall stones and renal congestion.

Evening Primrose

Parts used: oil from seed

Indications : hormonal, works on nervous system and on reproductive system. Used for M.S.

Thought for the Day

Who looks not cannot find,
who dares not cannot win.

Thought for the Day

Do nothing in secret,
for time sees and hears all things
and reveals all things.

Parsley

Parts used: all

Indications: diuretic and cleanser

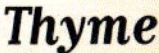

Thyme

Parts used: leaves

Indications: natural antibiotic and antiseptic

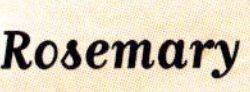

Rosemary

Parts used: Leaves

Indications: diuretic, reviver

Sage

Parts used: leaves

Indications : hormonal, contains a natural oestrogen helps with menopause problems.

Burdock

Parts used: root

Indications: skin problems, acne, eczema, psoriasis, detox and cleanses the blood.

Garlic

Borage

Parts used: oil extract from seed

Indications: anti-aging, wrinkles, dry skin

Garlic

Indications: natural antibiotic

Black currant

Indications: Vitamin C

Devils Claw

Parts used: Root

Indications: rheumatism, arthritis

Thought for the Day

Those who forget their parents
are a stream without water,
a tree without roots.

Echinacea

Parts used: Flowers & Leaves

Indications: Natural antiseptic and antibiotic

Dill

Parts used : all parts, seeds, flowers and leaves

Feverfew

Parts used: Leaves

Indications: Relieves migraine

Feverfew

White Willow

Indications: The aspirin was derived from willow

Marsh Mallow

Parts used: Leaves - infused in tea

Indications: Used for cystitis

Horse Radish

Parts used: root

Indications: aids digestion

Aloe Vera

Parts used: Juice

Indications: Used as creams and diluted as drinks for intestinal disorders

Lemon Verbena

Parts used: Leaves

Indications: A restful tea

Marigold

Marigold

Parts used: Flowers

Indications: Used in creams for skin

Holy thistle

Parts used: fruit

Indications: used for bleeding, sluggish liver

Cascara

Parts used: bark

Indications: softens the bowel movement

Fennel — Coriander – Aniseed (The 3 warmers)

Parts used: fruit

Indications: digestive upsets, colitis (inflammation of the bowel) expectorant

Ginger

Parts used: root

Indications: well known for its ease on the digestive system

Senna

Parts used: leaf

Indications: constipation

Ginseng

Parts used: root

Indications: stress, fatigue, to increase physical energy, ageing

Thought for the Day

Think health and you will achieve health.

Fenugreek

Parts used: seed

Indications: detox and acne

Royal Jelly

Indications: fatigue, convalescence, depression, anxiety, ageing, immune stimulant.

Propolis

Indications: immune system stimulant, fatigue

Spirulina

Parts used: whole plant

Indications: nutritional, proteins, vitamins and minerals

Golden seal

Parts used: rhizome

Indications: anti-inflammatory, aids digestion, heals mucous membrane

Lavender

Slippery elm

Parts used: inside bark

Indications: aids stomach complaints, laxative

Caraway

Parts used: seed

Indications: digestive

Wild Yam

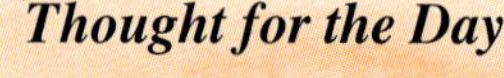

Thought for the Day

It is stern self-discipline that is at the base of all good health.

Clove

Parts used: buds

Indications: antiseptic, anti-inflammatory, analgesic, anti-parasitic

Sunflower

Parts used:

Indications:

Lavender

Parts used: flowers, made into essential oils

Indications: anti-biotic, anti-inflammatory, relaxant in massage, pure lavender oil eases the pain of burns, <u>avoid in pregnancy</u>

Mint

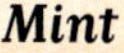

Mint

Parts used: leaf

Indications: digestive, infuse as a tea to aid digestion, antiseptic, anti-inflammatory

Basil

Parts used: leaves

Indications: essential oil, anti-depressant, antiseptic, expectorant, <u>do not use in pregnancy</u>

Oregano

Parts used:

Indications: antiseptic, used in Italian cooking, also as infusion in tea for headaches, coughs, nervous exhaustion

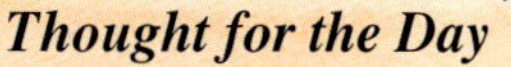

Thought for the Day

Our job is not to see through one another but to see one another through

Lerne the hygh and mervlous Vertue of herbs

Knowe how inestimable a preservative

to the health of man God hath provided

growying every day at our hande,

use the effects with reverence,

and give thanks to the maker celestyall.

Geopathic Stress

Thought for the Day

Give not from the top of your purse but from the bottom of your heart.

Geopathic stress is earth energies which cause disturbance in the body and the immune system. These are caused by underground water, overhead pylons, and magnetic rays from mobile phones and also from modern technology.

These stress areas can cause serious or severe damage to immune systems, particularly in a sleep area, where we spend the longest time. Houses which are situated over wells have tributaries from those wells running underneath the houses. These can be found by a good diviner and by simply moving furniture or bed to a safer area releases the body from the stress caused by flowing or stagnated water underneath the areas of living. Overhead pylons – if you venture into an area where there are overhead pylons you can hear the buzz, which can be very uncomfortable. It is recorded that the milk yield in cows grazing in an area where there are pylons is reduced. It is also a well known fact that where you see cattle resting is an area free from geopathic stress.
There is a very good book available called 'Are you sleeping in a safe place?'. It is becoming evermore detailed so I am going to give you the website of Dulwich Health Society, for those of you who wish to learn more, www.dulwichhealth.co.uk.

Electromagnetic Stress

Summary

Your health is your wealth and in your hands. It takes discipline to do this, but the feeling of well being is just wonderful and when you feel well you can cope with anything and everything.

So to do this:

- *Exercise and fresh air, particularly when the days are shorter.*
- *Good diet is essential. Cut out all additives and preservatives, colourings, flavourings etc.*

In other words, cut out packets, dried foods which contain these, plus soft drinks. Cook fresh food, particularly bread. The fresh yeast bread, rolls and croissants are baked with fast growing yeast and are causing a major digestive problem for all. Don't forget, all disease starts in an unclean colon. The photo of the yeast is in the Digestive System chapter - I grew that on a slice of yeast bread. It just got bigger and bigger and the spores were floating off it. It then began to turn black, so I decided to photograph it and discard it because the odour was becoming unpleasant.

That, folks, is what is growing in your intestine and creates total discomfort, bloating, wind causing an unsocial odour and eventually mal-absorption of vitamins and minerals. Eventually energy goes down, tiredness and irritability set in - the poor body is in total discomfort.

As I said earlier, babies are now being born with this condition carried through from the umbilical cord in utero.

The other symptoms are:

- *Itchy skin - but no obvious sign of rash.*
- *Fuzzy brain - my description for the feeling in the head of 'fog'.*
- *Inability to concentrate.*
- *Weight gain*
- *Fluid*

The good news as many of you know is that this can all be cleaned.

Strict yeast and sugar free diet for 4-6 weeks, herbs, homeopathy and flower therapies to clean up the undesirables inside, including parasitic infection - which is very common.

I don't approve of on-going diets with the exception of celiac and diabetic, because you are instructing your brain not to accept certain foods. A short couple of weeks a couple of times a year, plus cleaning liver, kidneys, digestive system with remedies as close to nature as possible.

Herbs are gifts from nature but to be used in some cases with caution - refer to suggested reading.

Sean Boylan is one of our most renowned herbalists. He lives in County Meath and I attended him back in the 70's when I had severe colitis - a very good reason why today my work is all about cleaning the digestive tract.

*Follow your diet with a few sessions of reflexology and daily exercise. You who have done this, know the results, quality of life returns and then you can eat everything in moderation, **but** your stomach will then let you know what it does not like and you will feel it.*

The biggest offenders are wheat which is heavily sprayed and your poor liver sorts out the chemicals and they reside there. Substitute for wheat: maize meal, rice flour, spelt flour, buckwheat flour (rhubarb family), and Millet. All are much easier to digest than wheat.

Dairy produce in moderation - lactose intolerance is a big problem. Milk is not what it used to be on Grandmothers farm, because there was no such thing as fertiliser, grass was green and full of herbs.

Potato: Before the potato was domesticated it was deadly nightshade poison family. This includes tomato, aubergine, peppers and tobacco.

If the body does not like it, it causes 'itis', inflammation, so withdraw it if you have pains in your joints.

Itis is inflammation, find the cause and it can be treated and deleted from your system, you can reach your senior years upright, mobile and in good shape, that is what you call "quality of life".

Diet for your heart, having all medical checks, in case of disease or narrowing of arteries. Exercise is the big one, get the circulation moving, never sit for long, dance, walk, skip, just do whatever you enjoy, as well as your heart, exercise keeps the circulation moving around the body and keeps your muscles in good shape too.

It is your body, look after it, treasure it and it will respond.

A Mediterranean style diet, low in fats and dairy but a healthy combination of proteins, fat and carbohydrates, a glass of good red wine is indicated too, whiskey is allowed - it is a vaso dilator (opens up the arteries) and so sends the blood speeding around the body, including the brain, very important for healthy brain function. Do not mix whiskey and wine, the Grape and Grain do not do well together.

Keep everything moving - the answer to a happy, healthy, joyful, contented body. The effects will be noticeable to all but mostly to you.

Mental, emotional and physical health is the outcome of discipline, correct diet and exercise.

Sanskrit Hymn

Look to this day for it is life,
The very life of life.
In its brief course lie all
The realities and truths of existence –
The joy of growth,
The splendour of action,
The glory of power!
For yesterday is but a memory
And tomorrow is only a vision,
But today well lived makes every yesterday
A memory of happiness,
And every tomorrow a vision of hope.
Look well, therefore, to this day.

and.....

Thought for the Day

Happiness is as a butterfly, which, when pursued, is always beyond your grasp, but which, if you will sit down quietly, may alight on you.

Nathaniel Hawthorne (1804-1864)

An Old Irish Proverb

May the road rise to meet you
May the wind be always at your back
May the sun shine warm upon your face
The rain fall soft upon your fields
and until we meet again
May your God hold you in the palm of His hand

Thoughtfully yours
Elizabeth Anne Shaw

Bibliography

Folk Medicine, *D.C. Jarvis M.D., Pan Books London & Sydney*

Crystal Healing, *Edmund Harold, Greenhouse Pub., Pty Ltd., Richmond, Victoria, Australia*

Bio Force Vademecum, *Dr. Alfred Vogel, Bioforc U.K. Ltd., Olympic Business Park, Drybridge Rd., Dundonald, Ayrshire, Scotland, KA2 9BE*

Sona Herbal Products, *very useful informative booklet, Sona@iol.ie, your local health shop or 01 4515087*

Naturalife Health Ltd., *Rathnew, Co. Wicklow, www.naturalife.ie, 0404 62444*

Mind and Body, *The Mind Alive Encyclopedia, Chartwell Books Inc., 110 Enterprise Ave., Secausus, New Jersey, 07094*

The Way Your Body Works, *Dr. Bernard Stonehouse, Crown Pub. Inc., New York*

Herbally Yours, *Penny C. Royal, Sound Nutrition, 55 South 100 East, Payson, UTAH, 84651*

Zen Soup, *Laurence G. Boldt, Penguin Group, Penguin Putnam Inc., 375 Hudson Street, New York, 10014, USA*

Managing Stress, *Jere E. Yates, Amacon, 135 West 50th Street, New York, NY 10020*

Herbal Remedies, *Sona Nutrition Ltd., sona@iol.ie*

Anatomy Colouring Book, *Wynn Kaptt/Laurence M. Elson/Harper & Row Pub., 10 East 53rd, New York, NY 10022*

The Skeletal & Muscular Systems, *Glen F. Bastian, Harper Collins College Publishers*

Herbal Remedies, *Tamara Kircher & Penny Lowery, Peter Albright M.D., Quantum Books Ltd., 6 Blundell St., London N79BH*

See Inside Your Body, *Katie Daynes & Colin King, Dr. Zoe Fritz, MBBS, MRCP, Usbourne Publishing Ltd., www.usbourne.com*

Butterflies & Moths, *John Still, Harper Collins Pub. Ltd., 77-85 Fulham Palace Rd., London, W68JB, www.collins.co.uk*

The Famous Butterflies Cards, *Heritage Playing Card Co., Toy & Game Co. Ltd.*

The Body Atlas, *Giuliano Foraari, Dorling Kindesley Ltd., 9 Henrietta St., London WC2E 8PS, England*

Herb & Spice, *Jill Norman, Dorling Kindersley Ltd.,*

A Country Harvest, *Pamela Michael, Peerage Books, 59 Grosvenor St., London W1*

Bach Flower Remedies, *Pictorial Ref. Cards, Oxfordshire OX14 5JX, UK*

A Pictorial Handbook of Anatomy & Physiology, *Dr. James Bevin, Mitchell Beazley, Octopus Pub. Group Ltd., 2-4 Heron Quays, London, E14 4JP, England*

A-Z of Natural Remedies, *Amanda Sandeman, Blitz Editions Orbis Publishing Ltd., Bookmart Ltd., Desford Rd., Enderby, Leicester, LE95AD, UK*

Alzheimers Challenged & Conquered, *Louis Blank, Foulsham, The Publishing House, Bennetts Close, Chippenham, Berks, SLI 5AP, England*

The Practice of Aromatherapy, *Dr. Jan Valnet, C.W. Daniel Co. Ltd., 1 Church Path, Saffron Walden, Essex, England*

It's All In Your Head, Mercury, Amalgams & Illness, *Dr. Hal A. Muggins, Avery Pub. Group Inc., Garden City Park, New York, USA*

The Family Guide to Homeopathy, *Dr. Andrew Lockie, Penguin Books Ltd., 27 Wrights Lane, London, W8 5T2, England*

The Art of Aromatherapy, *Robert Tisserand, C.W. Daniel Co. Ltd., 1 Church Path, Saffron Walden, Essex CB10 IJP, England*

The Clinical Science of Mineral Therapy, *Leslie Fisher, Dee Why Printing Works Pty Ltd., Sydney*

Herbs: Pocket Encyclopedia, *Lesley Bremness, Dorling Kindersley Ltd., 9 Henrietta St., London WC2E 8PS, England*

A Vision of Eden, *Marianne North, Webb & Bower Pub. Ltd., 33 Southernhay East, Exeter, Devon, EX1 INS*

Simple Healing with Herbs, *Penelope Ody, Bounty Books, Octopus Pub. Group Ltd., 2-4 Heron Quays, London, E14 4JP*

Food Allergies & Environmental Illness, *Dr. Keith Mumby, Harper-Collins Pub., 77-85 Fulham Palace Rd., Hammersmith, London, W6 8JB*

N.D.D.T.Y., www.wexusmagazine.com

The Sayings of White Eagle, The Quiet Mind

Something Special, *Litchfield Lodge, Frampton Rd., Boston, Lincs, PE 20INY*

The Green Pharmacy, *Dr. James A. Dure, Index Books Ltd.*

The Famous Book of Herbs, *Heath & Heather, St. Aibans, 1931*

Culpepper's Complete Herbal, *W. Foulsham & Co. Ltd., London*

Joseph Corvo's Zone Therapy, *Century Books, London*

Random Acts of Kindness, *Conani Press, 2550 Ninth St. Suit 101, Berkely, CA. 94710*

Suggested Reading

Traditional Home & Herbal Remedies, *Jan de Vries*

Sona Herbal Products, *very informative booklet available from your health shop, sona@iol.ie*

The Reflexology Handbook, *Laura Norman with Thomas Cowan, Judy Piatrus Publishing Ltd., 5 Windmill Street, London W1*

The Original Works of Eunice D. Ingnam, *Ingham Pub. Inc., Saint Petersburg, Florida, USA*

Healing with Herbal Juices, *Siegfried Gursche, Alive Books, PO Box 80055, Burnaby BC, Canada VSH 3X1*

The Clinical Science of Mineral Therapy, *Leslie Fisher, Dee Why Printing Works PTY Ltd., Sydney, Australia*

A-Z of Natural Remedies

D.K. Pocket Encyclopedia - Herbs

A Country Harvest *by Pamela Michael, Peerage Books*

Food Allergies An Environmental Illness, *Dr. Keith Mumby*

The Green Pharmacy, *Dr. James A. Dure, Index Books Ltd.*

Culpepper's Complete Herbal, *W. Foulsham & Co. Ltd., London*

Joseph Corvo's Zone Therapy, *Century Books, London*

Aculife, *+353 1 460 4962 or visit at www.aculife-ireland.com or www.aculife.co.uk*

A Pictorial Handbook of Anatomy & Physiology, *Dr. James Bevin, Mitchell Beazley, Octopus Pub. Group Ltd., 2-4 Heron Quays, London, E14 4JP, England.*